AFTER MARRIAGE
ENDS

NEW PERSPECTIVES ON FAMILY

Published in cooperation with the National Council on Family Relations

NCFR

Series Editor: **Linda Thompson**
University of Wisconsin, Madison

Books appearing in New Perspectives on Family are either single- or multiple-authored volumes or concisely edited books of original articles on focused topics within the broad field of marriage and family. Books can be reports of significant research, innovations in methodology, treatises on family theory, or syntheses of current knowledge in a subfield of the discipline. Each volume meets the highest academic standards and makes a substantial contribution to our knowledge of marriage and family.

SINGLES: Myths and Realities, *Leonard Cargan and Matthew Melko*

THE CHILDBEARING DECISION: Fertility Attitudes and Behavior,
Greer Litton Fox, ed.

AT HOME AND AT WORK: The Family's Allocation of Labor,
Michael Geerken and Walter R. Gove

PREVENTION IN FAMILY SERVICES: Approaches to Family Wellness,
David R. Mace, ed.

WORKING WIVES/WORKING HUSBANDS, *Joseph H. Pleck*

THE WARMTH DIMENSION: Foundations of Parental Acceptance-Rejection Theory,
Ronald P. Rohner

FAMILIES AND SOCIAL NETWORKS, *Robert M. Milardo, ed.*

FAMILIES AND ECONOMIC DISTRESS: Coping Strategies and Social Policy,
Patricia Voydanoff and Linda C. Majka, eds.

SINGLE WOMEN/FAMILY TIES: Life Histories of Older Women,
Katherine R. Allen

FAMILY VARIABLES: Conceptualization, Measurement, and Use
Thomas W. Draper and Anastasios C. Marcos, eds.

THE SECOND CHILD: Family Transition and Adjustment
Robert B. Stewart, Jr.

AFTER MARRIAGE ENDS: Economic Consequences for Midlife Women
Leslie A. Morgan

Other volumes currently available from Sage and sponsored by NCFR:

THE SOCIAL WORLD OF OLD WOMEN: Management of Self-Identity,
Sarah H. Matthews

THE VIOLENT HOME, Updated Edition, *Richard J. Gelles*

SEX AND PREGNANCY IN ADOLESCENCE, *Melvin Zelnik, John F.
Kantner, and Kathleen Ford*

AFTER MARRIAGE ENDS

ENDS

ECONOMIC CONSEQUENCES for MidLife WOMEN

LesLie A. MORGAN

Published in cooperation with
the National Council on Family Relations

SAGE PUBLICATIONS
The International Professional Publishers
Newbury Park   London   New Delhi

Copyright © 1991 by Sage Publications, Inc.

For information address:

SAGE Publications, Inc.
2455 Teller Road
Newbury Park, California 91320

SAGE Publications Ltd.
6 Bonhill Street
London EC2A 4PU
United Kingdom

SAGE Publications India Pvt. Ltd.
M-32 Market
Greater Kailash I
New Delhi 110 048 India

Printed in the United States of America

Library of Congress Cataloging-in-Publication Data

Morgan, Leslie A.
    After marriage ends: economic consequences for midlife women /
Leslie A. Morgan.
        p.   cm. — (New perspectives on family)
    "Published in cooperation with the National Council on Family Relations."
    Includes bibliographical references (p.   ).
    ISBN 0-8039-3548-X (c). — ISBN 0-8039-3549-8
    1. Divorced Women—United States—Economic conditions. 2. Widows
—United States—Economic conditions. 3. Middle aged women—United
States — Ecomonic conditions. 4. Marriage—Economic aspects— United
States.   I. National Council on Family Relations. II. Title.
III. Series.
HQ834.M674 1991
306.88—dc20   90-19472
                                                                                  CIP

FIRST PRINTING, 1991

Sage Production Editor: Michelle R. Starika

Contents

Series Editor's Foreword

The study of the economic dependence of women in marriage has a long history. We have learned that the subject is not simple. General statements about women's poverty after divorce and their salvation through wage work or remarriage are misleading. Leslie Morgan's book demonstrates that the diversity and complexity of women's lives defy general statements. To illustrate life's complexity, Morgan offers a portrait of 15 years of one woman's marital transitions: "[She] was married in 1967, and subsequently separated, reconciled with her husband, again separated, divorced, remarried, and finally widowed." The women in this book—characteristic of midlife women in the United States—have dynamic lives: They move in and out of marriage, wage work, and poverty. Their incomes rise and fall. Such changing lives make us appreciate the difficulty of Morgan's task.

In *After Marriage Ends*, Morgan explores the economic protection of marriage among midlife women by comparing several marital transitions—separation, divorce, widowhood, and remarriage. Rather than simply compare the financial straits of women in different marital statuses, she follows the same women over several years. She considers the occurence, order, and timing of marital transitions, labor force participation, and financial well-being. She asks difficult questions: Why do some women founder financially when marriage ends, and some thrive? Does *how* a marriage ends matter to women's financial security? How do the circumstances and characteristics that predispose women to marital termination affect their financial situation after marriage ends? Are wage work and remarriage strategies women use to sustain or regain financial security and, if they are, do these strategies work? Leslie Morgan's answers are not simple; they are insightful.

It is Morgan's attention to the diversity and complexity of women's lives and her successful struggle with time and process that make this book worthy of sponsorship by the National Council on Family Relations. It is difficult for researchers to deal with such complex issues in journal articles. The NCFR-Sage Book Series provides scholars with the opportunity to present their thoughts and findings as a whole. This is useful for both authors and readers. Leslie Morgan's book brings coherence and clarity to our understanding of the economic protection of marriage.

—*Linda Thompson*

Preface

In September 1988 columnist Ellen Goodman described marriage as "a phase women go through," citing recent data on the high rate of mobility experienced by individuals moving sequentially through a variety of household forms and relationships in their lifetimes.

> It appears that women who once felt protected by marriage to a wage earner now feel a greater sense of what the pollsters like to call marginality.... [N]ow, married women increasingly worry about the economic long run . . . because women who work outside the home and those who work inside have some similar experience or consciousness of the need to support themselves.

This and many other popular press articles are beginning to discuss in a more systematic fashion the economic side of marriage. Still considered by many to be unsavory or, at least, unromantic, such discussions have been prompted by the recognition that marriage today does not imply the same level of security for women that has been true in earlier decades.

This book examines the consequences for women in midlife when their marriages end, focusing on the economic changes. Although the experiences of no two women are alike, research completed to date suggests that most women experience striking economic declines, forcing major changes in their lifestyles and those of their children. Most of the work on women in this age range has focused on divorce, but there are other forms of marital termination that disrupt marriages and the lives of women and their dependent children: widowhood and separation. Here a comparative approach is taken to the forms of marital termination to examine whether it is the type of ending that shapes economic outcomes (e.g., by determining the benefits to which one is entitled) or whether it is the fact of leaving marriage through whatever means that prompts the decline of economic fortunes.

Certainly the continued reliance on the wages of male breadwinners in families, encouraged by the sex-based wage gap and the assignment of child-care responsibilities primarily to women, means that the removal of the husband as a key player has striking effects on the incomes of wives and children. Yet changing expectations and policies increasingly portray women as able to be economically self-sufficient very quickly following the termination of a marital relationship.

Here data from a large national panel of women are used to examine what actually happens to these women and their families over the years following the end of a marriage. Although perhaps not shocking, the findings do confirm in great detail the nature and diversity of the changes experienced by midlife women when their marriages end, and some of the ways they respond to those changes.

The core of this book outlines the sometimes dramatic and socially significant changes occurring to women as they are separated, widowed, or divorced. Looking at the aggregate, however, sometimes permits us to overlook the very specific and poignant stories of individual women. These women muster all of their resources to deal with what are in some cases very dire economic outcomes from the termination of their marriages. Although that personal story is not the focus here, the fact that we are talking about changes in the lives of real women should remain an important focus throughout.

ACKNOWLEDGMENTS

As with any major project of this type, there are a variety of people to thank for assistance. First I would like to thank my colleagues and staff at the University of Maryland Baltimore County who have provided innumerable helps in the completion of the research. Special mention should be made of the past and present chairs of my department, David T. Lewis and Derek G. Gill, both of whom have been very supportive. I also want to thank the staff of Academic Computing Services (especially Jack Suess), who have helped me out of more than one bind. I greatly appreciate the efforts of series editor Linda Thompson, the two anonymous reviewers, and colleagues such as Gay Kitson and Natalie Sokoloff, whose helpful comments undoubtedly made this a much better book. And, of course, I'd like to thank Dan, who was consistently supportive throughout the lengthy time period I was "doing the book." Any remaining errors in methodology, findings, or interpretation are mine and reflect in no way on those who have been so generous in their assistance.

—*Leslie A. Morgan*

1

The Economics
of Marriage

In the contemporary United States marriage is interpreted primarily as an intensely important interpersonal relationship founded on the basis of romantic love and sustained by couple companionship, emotional and sexual intimacy, and the sharing of important life events, typically including child-rearing. Marriage, then, is defined as a centrally important social bond, with norms of privacy against the outside intervention of others, such as friends, family, and the state.

As appealing as this image remains, marriage is realistically an institution that operates on many social levels. The romantic light in which we describe marriage diverts attention from the fact that marriage is, among its many facets, an economic relationship that binds the married couple by legal regulations and social norms governing their economic duties as husband and wife. It is this economic relationship that serves as the starting and central point of this volume.

THE ECONOMIC BASIS
OF MARRIAGE

It takes only a little digging to uncover the economic dimension of marriage in various cultures and historical periods, including our own. One needs only to compare descriptions of arranged marriages, with dowries and bride wealth as part of the marital agreement, to see this economic side of the relationship as being more clearly emphasized and explicit in other times and places (Goode, 1963; Kaplan, 1985; Kuper, 1982; Prothro & Diab, 1974). Marriages frequently have been used to create economic and social alliances between families and often have involved the exchange of economically valuable goods. Although less explicit, the economic dimension of marriage is also far from absent in current U.S. society.

Here domestic relations laws governing marriage in the various states define the economic dimensions of the marital bond. These laws outline the duties of mutual economic support by spouses and the rules for determining ownership of property or wealth accumulated during a marriage (Gates, 1977). Yet, in focusing our interest on the socioemotional components of the marital relationship, we deemphasize this central and legally defined aspect of the marriage (Arendell, 1986). Today, even outside the boundaries of marriage, innovations such as prenuptial agreements seek to establish ownership of property brought into a marriage and "palimony" suits to define legally the economic rights of non-marital cohabiting couples (Weitzman, 1983).

Unfortunately it is when a marriage ends that the importance of the economic ties, and specifically the financial benefits of marriage to women, become apparent (Arendell, 1986; Bergmann, 1981; Gates, 1977; Weitzman, 1985). Examination of the available statistics on poverty rates makes this point with ease. Women are significantly more likely to be poor at any adult age than are men and face higher risks of ever experiencing poverty in their lifetimes (Holden, Burkhauser, & Myers, 1986). Further examination of statistics on poverty among women yields one startling result. Poverty for women is heavily concentrated among those who are widowed, divorced, and separated. The rate of poverty is disproportionately high among the female heads of single-parent households created either through nonmarital childbearing or divorce (Bahr, 1983; Hoffman, 1977; Mott & Moore, 1978), and among middle-aged and older women who have experienced some form of marital dissolution (U.S. Bureau of the Census, 1989). Thus, it appears that marriage provides economic protection to women, as demonstrated in national data in Table 1.1. Women who are currently least likely to fall below the poverty line are those of all ages who are married with a spouse present (Taeuber & Valdisera, 1986; U.S. Bureau of the Census, 1987c).

It is, however, not simply marital status differences that contribute to the variation in poverty levels shown in the table. Because divorces and separations tend to occur earlier in the life cycle, while widowhood tends to occur at more advanced ages, aggregate comparisons of the economic fortunes of women in these marital categories folds in the effects of varying cohort experience in earnings and the labor force, family life cycle stages, and so on. In other words, not all of the differences necessarily derive from effects of marital status alone. A range of other factors, including age, race, and

Table 1.1 Poverty Rates of Women (15 Years or Older) by Marital Status and Age, 1987

	% Poor
Married, Spouse Present (Total)	6.0
15-44	6.6
45-64	5.7
65+	6.0
Widowed (Total)	21.5
15-44	28.6
45-64	34.0
65+	20.0
Divorced (Total)	22.1
15-44	23.5
45-64	18.9
65+	23.9
Separated (Total)	44.1
15-44	47.5
45-64	39.6
65+	41.2

SOURCE: U.S. Bureau of the Census, 1989.

socioeconomic status, differentially shape the overall risks of poverty in each of these groups. Yet the marital status/poverty connection persists even if we control for many of these other traits (e.g., race, employment status, education, parity) that cut across the population of women (Dressel, 1988; Taeuber & Valdisera, 1986; U.S. Bureau of the Census, 1989).

The Issue: Consequences of Marital Termination for Economic Well-Being

The data on poverty suggest that moving from marriage to a formerly married status places women at risk of becoming poor. Both anecdotal evidence and research support the notion that women whose marriages end typically face a dramatic economic downturn, even if they are not plunged into poverty (Arendell, 1987). In addition, cross-sectional data show that women fare considerably worse than men after a marriage ends.

As Table 1.2 shows, men in all three postmarital groups have lower rates of poverty than women, with the gap especially wide for the separated. Total household income is also quite different for men and women among the widowed and divorced, paralleling variations in the poverty statistics. Under

Table 1.2 Economic Status of Adults (25-64 Years of Age) by Marital
Status and Sex, United States 1985

	%Poor[b]	Median Income
Widowed		
Men	18.2	$13,873
Women	24.0	$9,492
Divorced		
Men	11.4	$19,145
Women	22.3	$13,573
Separated		
Men	15.0	[a]
Women	42.4	[a]

SOURCE: U. S. Bureau of the Census, 1987b, 1987c.
a. Median incomes were not available by sex for separated individuals
b. Poverty figures represent the proportion below the poverty level defined by the government.

the current structure of family systems in the United States, marriage appears to afford women a level of economic protection from poverty unavailable to them outside its boundaries. Earnings of husbands still provide for families in a manner which women, living alone and/or with their children, typically find difficult to achieve. The departure from marriage thus seems to place women at risk of economic distress regardless of the manner in which the marriage ends.

Although a growing body of quality research documents the economic changes occurring for women after marriage ends, questions still remain. First, is the marital termination itself really responsible for reducing economic well-being among women after separation, widowhood, or divorce? A focal point of the debate is the direct effect of leaving marriage on economic well-being. It must be recognized that not all women face equal risks of separation, divorce, or widowhood. If in fact women who are more economically disadvantaged (poorer educational background, limited employment experience, minority ethnicity, low wages, and/or high unemployment) are more likely to become widowed, separated, or divorced, their financial plight might well reflect a gathering of these already disadvantaged women rather than simply the consequences of marital termination. Moreover, this problem of selectivity can be further exaggerated by selective remarriage if it removes relatively more of the socially or economically advantaged women from the ranks of the formerly married over time.

Related to this argument is one suggesting that the crux of the income problems experienced by formerly married women is nothing more than the combined consequence of sexism, racism, and ageism (Dressel, 1988). That is, women in the larger society are economically disadvantaged compared to men in access to quality employment opportunities. Marriage offers women the opportunity to partake of those gender-restricted advantages indirectly, through the incomes and benefits earned by their husbands. When a marriage ends by death, divorce, or separation, then, the woman is once again at the mercies of a system that constrains her chances for achieving a substantial income (Ozawa, 1989). In this view it is not marriage that is at fault, but rather the larger systems of inequality fostering poorer outcomes for women, especially women of color or those of advancing age.

In the chapters to follow we will examine these issues by looking directly at the changes in income, employment, and remarriage among women whose marriages end in midlife, in an effort to sort out the effects of departures from marriage from preexisting differences. Among the questions to be addressed are the following:

What are the consequences of separation, divorce, and widowhood on the economic well-being of midlife women?

Are the consequences the same for women regardless of how the marriage ended?

To what extent is the income status of formerly married women the result of marital termination as compared to prior economic standing, background traits, and selection factors?

What groups of women are especially likely to experience poverty or severe declines in their standard of living?

What are the prospects of formerly married women significantly improving their economic fortunes over time through participation in the labor force or via remarriage?

To explore the selection problem, we will both comparatively examine the women before their marriages end and look at how much their postmarital situations change compared to their individual circumstances during marriage.

Results of such comparisons have important implications for social policy. For example, if it is determined that women leaving marriage experience an elevated risk of poverty, are unable to achieve an adequate livelihood for their families from the labor force, and rely on remarriage as a solution to poverty, it would suggest the need for some significant changes in laws and social norms. Such findings would indicate basic, structural inequities that need to be addressed on a policy level, rather than simply leaving formerly married women to do the best they can in the marketplace. Marriage may, with both its formal and informal rules suggesting the dependency of wives, contribute to the overall level of income disadvantages.

Policies may also need to address problems that women have faced for much longer; those of being second class members of family units and of society. There is a long tradition in law and custom making women lesser partners in the marital relationship that persists despite growing educational and employment opportunities in the latter half of the twentieth century (Bianchi & Spain, 1986; Weitzman, 1983). This research addresses the role of marriage in this pattern of economic disadvantage.

BACKGROUND FOR THE CURRENT STUDY

Persuasive arguments have been mustered to suggest that it is the marital relationship and changes occurring during its tenure that economically disadvantage women. In contrast, a plausible argument can be put forward to suggest that the conditions in the larger society disadvantage all women, with marriage simply providing temporary insulation to women from these difficulties. Although it is not possible to test the relative importance of these macrolevel approaches with the data employed here, their concepts and assumptions provide the framework through which the consequences of marital termination are addressed. Both perspectives are described in greater detail below.

Economic Roles Within Marriage: The Risk of Women's Dependency

Economic roles within marriage are strongly related to the ideology of the family, which continues to provide assumptions regarding families and women's place within them. First and foremost, this ideology continues to place women in an economically dependent role within the family (Lopata & Brehm, 1986; Weitzman, 1983). This dependency, with roots in the Victorian cult of true womanhood, suggested that woman's place was in the home, insulated from the vulgarity of the economic marketplace (Cott, 1977). The world of paid employment had largely moved beyond the home after the Industrial Revolution, creating the possibility for women to separate themselves from that marketplace and rely on their husbands for financial support. This idealized version of the woman in the home, derived from the cult of true womanhood, only became a reality for women in middle- and upper-middle-class families in the late nineteenth and early twentieth centuries. It typically required the employment of poorer women as cooks, maids, and nannies. These less advantaged women, although unable to achieve the idealized lifestyle, were socialized that the full-time home-based activity of supervising servants and pursuing domestic arts was one to be held as a goal. In contrast, man's ideal role had become primarily oriented to the outside world, serving as provider to his family (Andersen, 1988).

Although times have certainly changed, the notion that women are economically dependent on their husbands has survived in both formal and informal fashion (Weitzman, 1983). Formally the presumption of wives' dependency is reflected in some laws and policies that continue to present the traditional distinction of roles: man the provider, woman the dependent (Lopata & Brehm, 1986; Weitzman, 1983). The economically valuable work women do within the household is not recognized as part of the nation's productivity or by generating benefits to housewives who become disabled ("Men and Women," 1979). States' domestic relations laws traditionally have provided greater economic protection for women than for men in marriage (and following it), due to their presumed economic dependency, and the Social Security system fails to reward working wives equitably for their earnings contributions to the household (Bahr, 1983; Gates, 1977; Lopata & Brehm, 1986; "Men and Women," 1979; Weitzman, 1983).

Even in contemporary American society the expectation that wives will be economically dependent in marriage is played out in personal and family decisions that often make it appear to be a self-fulfilling prophecy. Some women become economically dependent on their husbands during their marriages without having originally planned (or intended) to do so. Wives' economic independence erodes as a consequence of incremental decisions not to seek further education, or to take part-time rather than full-time work (Arendell, 1986).

Women also have been encouraged to prepare for jobs that will coordinate well with their "primary tasks" as mothers. They are also frequently steered toward jobs in which flexibility and fewer hours, both appealing to mothers of young children, are paired with lower salaries and limited career advancement (Rainwater, 1980). Because of these practices, some charge that women have "chosen" to remain in sex-segregated employment and forgo the higher rewards of other, male dominated occupations. Although sex segregation is diminishing slowly (Bianchi & Rytina, 1986; Sokoloff, 1988), the family structure that encourages at least some of that segregation through unequal division of household work and child-rearing duties remains in force (Crossman & Edmonson, 1985).

The activities involved in being a "good mother" can themselves diminish a woman's capability to provide for herself and her children through employment (Hewlett, 1986). One major constraint on women's competitiveness in the labor force is the limited availability of affordable, high quality child care. The high costs of purchasing such care, typically from other women, may make employment "too expensive" considering the average woman's relatively low wages (Sidel, 1986), and may promote more women staying at home full-time.

Informally women have continued to be socialized to place family first and involvement in the paid economy second, and to act in ways consistent with those expectations (Hewlett, 1986). For example, a wife might forgo further education herself in order to support her husband's education, which is likely to economically benefit them both in the future (Peterson, 1989). The necessity of having someone available to provide care for children during preschool years, after school, or in case of emergency has encouraged many women to choose less prestigious and less well-paying jobs that provide this greater flexibility (Rainwater, 1980). The gender-based nature of this hierarchy of interests is reflected in the grudging understanding of an employer when a woman takes time off work due to the illness of her child, although perhaps being less cooperative with a father taking time off under similar circumstances.

Some authors argue that the forces encouraging women to place the family first and other roles—including employment—second, is still quite strong today (Chodorow, 1978; Hewlett, 1986). The beliefs instilled in women and the structural realities of employment, Hewlett (1986) contends, continue to prevent mothers from taking full roles in the labor force. Women are socialized to value and receive encouragement toward participation in the essential functioning of the family, which society chooses not to recognize as economically valuable work. These priorities require some level of continued economic dependence on husbands' earnings, even among women who are employed.

Men, in contrast, are prepared for and expected to maintain full-time involvement in the paid economy. This involvement, in turn, largely fulfills their responsibilities to the family by providing economically for its needs (Voydanoff, 1987). Men who are employed other than full-time, however, are still called upon to provide some excuse or explanation, such as physical disability, for their behavior (Howards, Brehm, & Nagi, 1980).

Given the fact that men still earn more than women in the paid economy, and that we find a parallel earnings gap in the great majority of married couples, such decisions are rational ones in economic terms (Berch, 1982). For a wife to defer her own earnings in favor of her husband's (and eventually her children's) makes financial sense for the entire family, and provides a greater net benefit to everyone involved. Such decisions, however, are rational only as long as the marriage lasts (Bergmann, 1981). It is ironic that the occupational choices that women have been encouraged to make in order to benefit their families have often been the same decisions that have disadvantaged their children and themselves once the marriage ends through death, divorce, or separation (Arendell, 1986).

The result of these decisions is a smaller paycheck or a smaller potential earnings level for the wife (Bahr, 1983). In addition, most women take some time out from the labor force for childbearing and child-rearing, albeit less now than in the recent past (Bianchi & Spain, 1986). Women who opt to raise their children full-time find their job skills become increasingly obsolete with lengthy interruptions. Such interruptions diminish employability and long-range earnings capacity (O'Rand & Landerman, 1984; VanVelsor & O'Rand, 1984). Interrupted working careers for wives, which may be required in order to have children, may also serve to validate employers' assumptions that a woman worker will terminate her employment in favor of childbearing, making her seem a less favorable risk for training or promotion. Women often return to work as children grow older, but frequently the motivation will be to benefit the family, such as in earning college tuition, rather than building her own career.

Although the economic dependency of women in the family may grow incrementally, decision by decision, the risks of such dependency are high given the absence of economic guarantees in the marital relationship (Bergmann, 1981; Crossman & Edmonson, 1985). This pattern of dependency has serious and unintended outcomes if the marriage ends and the former wife is called upon to provide economically for herself and her children.

According to human capital theory, individuals develop characteristics that endow them with value, "human capital," which makes them more attractive to employers. The larger the available human capital individuals bring to the search for employment, the more likely they are to locate work and the more able they are to command jobs with high salaries and benefits. Human capital is more or less a commodity that individuals may engender through education, specific skills or talents, or experience, primarily in the labor force. Presumably there is a more or less direct translation of human capital into employability and returns from employment (Becker, 1973, 1974, 1975; Becker, Landes, & Michel, 1976; Peterson, 1989). For a long time research on factors included in human capital (i.e., education, work experience) has shown them to affect rates of employment, occupational status, and income. Yet human capital does not seem to explain a range of disparities that persist by marital status, race, gender, and age (see Bianchi & Spain, 1986; Peterson, 1989).

The linkage of human capital theory to the economic disadvantage of women following termination of marriage is a clear one. Simply, during marriage women have been encouraged to take actions and make decisions that reduce their individual human capital. By interrupting employment for child-rearing, taking part-time or less skilled work to accommodate family demands, or failing to seek advanced education in the interests of the family, individual women reduce their human capital. Women, through the institution of marriage, are able to share the higher wages, benefits and job security engendered by their husbands' human capital. The married lifestyle of the majority of adults thus could be interpreted as protective of women, limiting their income-generating responsibility and also providing couples with the time and opportunity to bear and rear children. This means, however, that once marriage ends former wives are less able to effectively compete in the outside economy. Work is more difficult to find and it may be of a less skilled or poorly compensated variety when it is located. In contrast, women who have been more heavily involved in education and employment during marriage would, if the human capital theory is correct, fare better than their "displaced homemaker" counterparts.

Inequity for Women in the Larger Economy

The second relevant perspective is that of gender discrimination. This includes both gender segregation in access to jobs and direct discrimination in wages or promotions by employers. Gender discrimination argues that regardless of the level of human capital accumulated by an individual, women will gain lesser returns than will men. These disadvantages are further magnified for individuals who experience the multiple jeopardy of also being members of ethnic/racial minorities or being "older workers."

Despite growth in educational opportunities for women and the tremendous expansion in the numbers of women in the labor force in recent decades (see Bianchi & Rytina, 1986), the evidence shows that opportunities for men and women remain unequal. Employment opportunities for women in the United States are circumscribed by the realities of the labor market, which continues to define women as secondary workers (Corcoran, Duncan, & Hill, 1984). Although the media portray women as approaching equality in the work place with respect to their occupational opportunities, career progress, and earnings and benefits, the realities for typical women are much more modest. This changing employment picture has influenced all women, but the most substantial changes in women's labor force behaviors and attitudes have occurred among younger, not midlife or older, women.

For example, women continue to experience marked wage differentials from males of equal education (Corcoran et al., 1984). Continuing sex segregation and sex discrimination in hiring and promotion limit the opportunity for women to earn incomes comparable to those of men by limiting their access to the higher paying jobs typically held by men (Bielby & Baron, 1986; Sokoloff, 1988). Evidence from the U.S. Census suggests that the growth in occupational opportunities for women at the highest levels has been much slower in coming than is commonly believed, regardless of growing educational equity between the sexes (Bielby & Baron, 1986; Sokoloff, 1988).

Women who need to return to work after the end of a marriage in which they had been economically dependent (Shaw, 1983), sometimes referred to as displaced homemakers, often face a difficult adjustment in reorienting themselves to the labor force (Lopata & Norr, 1980). For these women financial self-sufficiency had not been part of the plan, and the ending of their marriages came as an unpleasant and unanticipated shock (Weitzman, 1985). These unplanned careers, as Shaw has called them, often fly in the face of long-term plans of midlife women that included doing household work and child care as their primary activities (Shaw, 1983). Even though their skills may be obsolete and their educations inadequate to find lucrative employment, the domestic relations laws and judges in many states now assume that most divorcing displaced homemakers are able to compete for jobs that will make them self-sufficient in a relatively short time after divorce (Arendell, 1986; Weitzman, 1985).

The effects of continuing gender discrimination in the economy are not, it should be emphasized, restricted to displaced homemakers. Even where both members of a married couple are employed, loss of the earnings of a husband upon death or divorce presents a major financial blow to the household. If couples were earning equivalent salaries, which is seldom the case, each would experience a 50% decline in income as the marriage ends, with possible adjustment as various income support systems engage. Most typically, because men's earnings continue to outstrip those of women, it is the husband who earns the bulk of the household income. In these households the end of marriage means reduction from two incomes to one, typically leaving the wife with her smaller paycheck and perhaps some form of outside support (Pett & Vaughn-Cole, 1986).

Brewer (1988) and Dressel (1988) both suggest that women of color and those from disadvantaged backgrounds experience higher risks of poverty even during marriage, and are much more likely to find themselves poor once marriage ends. Already having spent a married life precariously close to the brink of poverty, many minority and lower class women find themselves pushed over the edge when their marriages end. The combined disadvantages of gender, race, and class diminish their opportunities to provide adequately for themselves and their children. Thus it is when women leave marriage that they lose their link to the opportunities that remain restricted to men and the benefits that derive from those opportunities. Formerly married women simply return to the ranks of the disadvantaged, without the economic protection of marriage.

This approach suggests that because of the remaining inequities in the labor market (sex segregation, wage inequities) and in the family system (differential responsibilities for children and household work, no credit for the economic contribution of household work) that have been structured into the system of gender roles, marriage becomes the only means of ensuring income security for themselves and their children. Marriage thus becomes a necessity for the majority of women to guarantee their economic well-being.

If marriage is a necessity, women who are no longer married might experience pressures other than individual choice to seek new marriage partners or to accept a spouse who is less pleasing (Ambert, 1983). This would make marriage a coercive institution for women, required if they are to minimize the risks of becoming poor.

POLICIES AFFECTING WOMEN AFTER MARRIAGE

Former wives are often shocked to discover that the economic support system they presumed to be waiting for them after marriage may be nonexistent. The laws and policies pertaining to income supports for widowed, separated, and divorced women have evolved somewhat independently from each other and have been subject to some important changes in recent years. It is fairly easy to discuss the divorced and widowed, for whom clear legal and policy provisions exist, but less simple to discuss the situation of the separated. For separated couples situations vary because their legal status may or may not be formalized, and the law often views separation as a transitional status on the path to divorce. Our focus in this section, therefore, is on widowed and divorced women as these different systems affect their economic well-being.

Some of the ambivalence with regard to financial support for formerly married women can be seen in the provisions of transfer programs for divorced and widowed women. Policies make important distinctions between women in terms of whether the marriage ended by divorce or death of the spouse. Programs and policies also operate under varied auspices (local, state, and federal government; various private agencies) and often reflect some very basic assumptions regarding the needs and "place in society" of women who are widowed or divorced. In the case of both widowed and divorced women, income support systems with their many flaws and loopholes have been conditional on the woman's role as a caregiving parent and, in the recent past, her presumed inability to be economically self-sufficient while caring for her children (Kamerman & Kahn, 1988; Lopata & Brehm, 1986). Some of these programs also bear the stigma of "welfare," potentially reducing participation and providing for these households at much lower levels than had been the case during marriage (Sidel, 1986).

Widows have been presumed to a substantial degree to have been dependent wives deserving of societal protection from the consequences of widowhood (Lopata & Brehm, 1986). The loss of a woman's spouse and termination of the economic bargain he made to provide for her support are viewed as not the widow's fault—so she deserves consideration and benefits from the larger society (Kamerman & Kahn, 1988). The extension of the Social Security system shortly after its inception to provide for dependents of workers reflected this major change in orientation. This modification formally recognized the economic dependence of women and children on a worker who might die, and society's responsibility toward them (Lopata & Brehm, 1986).

Widows continue to be defined as justifiably needy, and most can count on some benefits from Social Security. These benefits, however, are not universally awarded, but are received only if the widow meets eligibility criteria (Lopata & Brehm, 1986). Widows may draw benefits from their late husbands' earnings record if one of two qualifying statuses holds. First, they may have benefits as widowed wives if they are of "retirement" age, considered to be 60 or older. Alternatively, widowed mothers also may receive benefits from Social Security for themselves and their dependent offspring by virtue of their child care responsibilities. These benefits are, however, subject to an earnings test that reduces the benefits by $1.00 for every $2.00 earned above a specified ceiling, set at $6,120 for 1988 (Mallan, 1975).[1]

Women with moderate to high earnings may find that any supplement to their paychecks expected from Social Security is slashed by this earnings test, and benefit amounts typically do not replace the lost earnings of their husbands. For younger widows (less than 60 years of age) with no dependent children, however, there is no Social Security support, based on the assumption that the widow will either work to support herself or remarry.

In contrast, divorce is viewed as a voluntary ending to marriage allowing society to consider the role of fault for the failure in providing income support. In the past, divorced women often were characterized as "alimony drones," marrying and divorcing men but continuing to sit at home and do nothing but collect checks from hapless ex-husbands. Popular media reinforced the notion that men were impoverished by alimony and that women lived lives of comfort based on their lifetime support from ex-husbands (Weitzman, 1985). Recent research has concluded, however, that only a minority (14%-15%) of divorced women were ever awarded alimony and that most have not actually received all of the alimony that courts had awarded (Bahr, 1983; Gates, 1977). Middle- or upper-middle-class women, and especially those whose marriages had lasted many years, are more likely to be granted alimony (Weitzman, 1985), whereas working-class or poor women and those with more average length of marriage before divorce (less than 10 years) often are not awarded this type of support.

Divorced women have always been more likely to be awarded support for their children than for themselves (Kitson, Babri, & Roach et al., 1985). Receipt of neither alimony nor child support has been reliable, so that divorced women and their offspring could not count on that income for their survival (Weiss, 1984). Usually divorced women were awarded only child support, because their husbands did not earn sufficient income to continue supporting ex-wives. And, as Weitzman (1985) points out, judges have been hesitant to assign too high a proportion of the salary of a man to the support of a former wife and children, since he might wish to remarry and have a second family.

Changes in educational and employment patterns over the last few decades have served as a rationale for changes in the provisions for income supports to divorced women (Lopata & Brehm, 1986; Weitzman, 1985). Some of the policy changes, such as no-fault divorce, have financially harmed the average divorced woman in unanticipated ways (Weitzman, 1985). As a consequence of these recent changes, alimony or spousal support is increasingly viewed by the courts as a temporary benefit until a woman can (presumably) become self-sufficient through employment (Bahr, 1983;

Welch & Price-Bonham, 1984; Weitzman, 1985). Child support, child custody, and alimony are all increasingly viewed in nongendered and no-fault terms in the law, even though awards tend to follow somewhat traditional patterns (Freed & Walker, 1988). Thus the primary breadwinner for the couple or family may be required to transfer funds to the other spouse, regardless of who that individual is or of any private agreements during marriage. Typically this still means that a husband is held responsible for supporting his offspring and may be required to support his former spouse for some limited period of time.

Thus movement toward "no fault" divorce has resulted in substantial reductions in the support provided by husbands to their former wives and in the overall amount of the couples' assets awarded to the wife (Weitzman, 1985). Research has shown that the property settlements associated with no-fault divorces are less advantageous to the wife than had been the case under the adversarial system, with the wife now typically receiving half of the family assets including half of the family home (Arendell, 1987; Weitzman, 1985). The home is typically the largest asset of couples getting divorced, and the no-fault provision often requires that it be sold in order to divide assets down the middle. This removes a major resource, the family home, previously awarded to most divorcing women to enable them to continue raising their children with minimal disruption. This system of 50-50 property settlement also does not take into account that the former wife typically has custody of the children, which increases the real costs of living and the risks of falling into poverty once income is reduced (Weitzman, 1985).

As Weitzman (1985) has pointed out, there is a much stronger expectation in the divorce courts of the appropriateness of continuing income support to women who have served many years in the homemaking role during marriage. Her work also suggests that the wife's long tenure in her marital role may be responsible for society's greater willingness to support widowed women, whose marriages are typically long. Whether the differences in public notions of the deservedness of support arise from the greater perceived capacity of the younger woman to become self-supporting, the length of marriage, per se, or both is difficult to tell (Weitzman, 1985).

In sum, although there still is considerable sentiment for providing financial assistance to a wife of many years when her marriage ends, either through public programs such as Social Security widow benefits or through payments from an ex-husband, there is increasing pressure toward self-sufficiency for younger and midlife women whose marriages end. These changes assume that adequate protections remain in place for those who entered marriage under the earlier "contract," who might not have adequately prepared for economic independence (Weitzman, 1985).

Case Histories

In order to see more clearly how some of these changes take shape over time as women are widowed, separated, or divorced, five case histories are presented here. The cases were randomly selected from the large set of data—National Longitudinal Surveys (NLS)—used in later chapters, covering the time period from 1967 to 1982. Here their characteristics, especially those pertaining to economic well-being, are described in somewhat greater detail. These cases demonstrate not only the diversity of women undergoing marital transitions, but also the wealth of longitudinal data for examining connections between the end of marriage, economic well-being, work, and family.

Coincidentally, four of the five women selected have extensive employment histories, rather than being classic displaced homemakers. Only one reported any health problem that would limit her work or other activities during her participation in the study, and none of them remarried during their participation through 1982. Other than these points of similarity, however, their circumstances varied considerably.

Case A: Ms. A, a white woman, entered the study at age 43, having married for the first and only time in 1948. She was subsequently widowed at the age of 53. She held moderate ideas about women's employment, agreeing that it is definitely all right for a woman to work if the family needs money or if she wants to and her husband approves. Ms. A drew the line, however, at women working when their husbands disapprove, labeling that definitely not acceptable.

When the study began in 1967 Ms. A was in a job that she had held since 1955, with annual earnings under $4,000. The family's overall income in 1966 was $11,800, made up entirely of the wages of the couple. In 1967 she reported two dependents, children between the ages of 14 and 17 years. Ms. A reported in 1971 that her family's financial situation was "worse off" than it had been in 1969, primarily due to poor business conditions. By 1971 one of her children had left home, and the other subsequently departed by 1972. After her husband died in 1974, Ms. A changed jobs, gaining slightly in income and reducing her typical work week by several hours. Ms. A dropped out of the sample as of the 1979 interview, leaving as an employed 55-year-old widow with no children at home.

Case B: Ms. B was a black woman who entered the NLS panel in 1967 at the age of 35. She was then in her second marriage, which had begun in 1966, having been previously divorced. She had a 9th grade education and gained no further education during the study. Demonstrating an unusual marital sequence, Ms. B separated from her second husband between 1974 and 1976 and subsequently became widowed between 1976 and 1977. Like the women in the other cases, she had not remarried by 1982, when she was age 50. Ms. B had also been actively employed throughout her adult life and continued that participation during her years in the NLS panel. Ms. B held very liberal views regarding women working, believing it was definitely all right for women to work even if their husbands disapproved. Ms. B reported income in 1967 of just over $3,000, but that exceeded the income she reported for her husband. Added to this is the fact that Ms. B reported seven dependents, all living at home and ranging in age from 1 year to adolescence. This poor income situation improved by 1969 when both she and her husband nearly doubled their earnings and one child had left home. Her financial situation continued to be volatile, however, moving from $12,000 of total family income in 1969 to only $350 of reported earnings between herself and her husband in 1971. By 1972 family income had again improved and they were supporting only four of their children at home, reducing the level of financial need. Family income continued to fluctuate, however, with Ms. B reporting no earned income in 1974 just prior to separating from her husband, nor for herself as a widow in 1977. She dropped out of the labor force around the time of her husband's death, when she listed her employment status as "other." In 1979 she reported herself to be keeping house for herself and her four children, but planning to retire at age 65. By 1981, however, she was back in the labor force, earning $6,000 and receiving benefits as a widow from Social Security. She reported that she had just enough income to get by.

Ms. B demonstrates the dynamic nature both of income and of marital status. Her conditions changed drastically when her second marriage ended, but apparently for this woman such drastic changes were not unusual. Further, some of the decline in her income was related to her own withdrawal from the labor force for reasons that are not clear.

Case C: Ms. C entered the panel at the age of 37 and was divorced two years later. She was a black woman with a high school education. Ms. C was also in her second marriage, begun in 1960. Unlike most of her peers, Ms. C strongly disagreed with women working, regardless of the conditions. Yet she herself was employed most of her adult life and during her panel participation. Ms. C reported earnings of $6,500 for herself and $8,000 for her husband in 1966, with one dependent child, age 3, to support. Following her divorce in 1969 she continued to work full-time with slightly improved earnings that constituted the total income received by the household in that year. No alimony or child support was received, but we do not know whether any such payments were awarded by the court. Ms. C's is a case in which divorce dramatically reduced income. After her divorce, however, her own wages improved, suggesting some recovery had occurred by her third post-divorce interview. By 1971 her earnings had improved to $8,500, but that was the only money coming into that household. Ms. C dropped out of the study in 1972, continuing to support herself and her child, who was then approximately 8 years of age, solely on her own income.

Case D: Ms. D entered the study at age 32, in her first and only marriage. She was separated between 1977 and 1979 and subsequently divorced between 1981 and 1982. She, too, was black but had an education equivalent to five years of college. Ms. D reported substantial earnings throughout her participation in the study, starting at $11,700 in 1966. Furthermore, her earnings typically outstripped those she reported for her husband. She approved of women working under all conditions, and reported herself to be a full-time employee throughout her panel participation in the same job she had held since 1955. There were two dependent children in the household in 1967, one age 1 year and the other of elementary school age. She reported their family's financial situation had improved by 1971 due to increasing income. Her husband reported no income in 1971, but her own earnings had increased to $17,000, maintaining their standard of living. The couple continued to have increasing earnings as their children grew, up until the point of their separation. When the husband's income was removed by separation in 1979, the total family income dropped from $64,000 to $45,000. Although this drop is significant, it in no way threatened the economic security of a family of three. In 1979, at the age of 44, Ms. D said she planned to retire at age 55, but continued working at least 40 hours a week and was earning $50,000 by the time she was divorced from her husband in 1981. Not surprisingly, she reported that this income level was more than adequate and that they always had money left over. Finally, in 1982 Ms. D reported herself to be retired and continuing to support her two children as the study period ended.

Case E: Ms. E began her participation in the NLS panel at the age of 40. She was a white woman, married only once in 1952, with a high school education. Unlike some other cases, Ms. E was strongly opposed to married women working, disagreeing strongly under most conditions and only disagreeing moderately when both the woman and her husband agree. Unlike the other cases, Ms. E was true to her attitudes, reporting herself to be keeping house at the time of the 1967 survey. She reported having worked a total of three years on a full-time basis since she was age 18.

In 1967 Ms. E and her husband had a preschooler (age 3) and two other children of elementary school age. The total family income reported for 1966 was $9,185, almost entirely from the wages of Mr. E. Between 1969 and 1971 Ms. E became a widow. Just after being widowed, Ms. E was continuing to keep house and care for her three children, reporting a total family income for the prior year (1968) of $5,570, a 40% income drop. By 1971 she reported her subjectively evaluated financial situation to be worse off even than it had been in 1969, primarily due to increasing expenses in the cost of living— yet her total family income had risen to just over $6,000 for 1971 and 1972. During this time she remained outside the labor force, keeping house for her three children. She received benefits from Social Security as a widowed mother and from a pension program associated with her late husband's employment. Until 1977 the composition of the household did not change, but their income situation improved, with a reported income of $12,129. This change was brought about by Ms. E taking a half-time job in spite of her report that her health limited the amount of employment she could undertake. Her oldest child left home by 1979 and a second left by 1981. Ms. E's foray into employment was brief, ending by 1981 when she reported herself to be unemployed. Ms. E ended her participation in the study as an unemployed widow of 55 with a dependent child still at home. In 1982 she still reported herself in financial distress, with a total reported income in the previous year of $3,189.

Undoubtedly her limited work experience and negative attitudes toward employment contributed to her pattern of mostly staying home with her young children. Ms. E is the more traditional widow whose reliance on income support programs, both public and private, was fairly high. Although they did not provide an ample income, she was ultimately unable to significantly augment this through her own employment, perhaps as a result of lack of work experience combined with her health limitations.

SUMMARY AND PREVIEW

We begin with more questions than answers. Certainly it appears that women are at significantly higher economic risk following marriage. The challenge is to disentangle the potential causes and clarify whether it is selection that shapes the profile of poverty we have seen, or whether it is departure from marriage that creates the context for economic risk. If departure from marriage is responsible, are the choices and decisions during marriage that reduce human capital among women accountable for their higher rates of poverty? Alternatively, is the disadvantaged status of women in the employment marketplace responsible, or is it a combination of these forces?

In the chapters to follow we will examine these issues in a very concrete fashion, using the experience of a large sample of women over a 15-year time span to observe widowhood, separation, and divorce and how they affect the economic fortunes and the adjustments made by a range of American women. Examination of truly comparable data on the transitions experienced by women undergoing widowhood, divorce, and separation can provide important evidence to address the research questions posed earlier.

The next chapter begins by reviewing in greater detail the research evidence regarding financial outcomes for separated, divorced, and widowed women. A focus of attention is the variation among women in the severity of outcomes they experience, and factors that shape these events. Following this, the next chapters examine original evidence from a large national study of women regarding changes brought about in their economic status by the end of marriage through separation, widowhood, or divorce. The third chapter describes the characteristics of the NLS sample of women just before their marriages end and compares them to women whose marriages remain intact. This examination of baseline traits permits us partially to determine whether the selection argument described earlier can be shown to be responsible for a significant part of the income disadvantage of formerly married women. Simply comparing the economic status of formerly married and still-married women runs the risk of including preexisting income or asset differences in the comparison.

The subsequent set of chapters (4 through 6 respectively) examine in great detail the changes in economic well-being, labor force modifications, and remarriage patterns of women whose marriages ended during the study. These chapters detail the similarities and differences across groups of midlife women leaving marriage and the forces that differentiate their experiences. Because this is a longitudinal study, time is a critical factor. Women who are separated, widowed, or divorced are grouped together as though they had all experienced their transitions out of marriage at the same time. With appropriate controls it is possible to examine them in several subsequent interviews to see how their lives and circumstances have changed.

The final chapter evaluates the evidence and suggests the implications for the future of women both inside and outside of marriage, including both personal and policy changes that may be essential to increasing the equity between the sexes and the economic security of formerly married women.

NOTE

1. Dollar amounts for the earnings test are regularly adjusted to reflect changes due to inflation. Recent changes (effective January, 1990) in the provisions of Social Security have modified the earnings test provision for those 65-69 years of age to reduce benefits by one dollar for every three dollars earned above the specified limit. This presumably enhances the motivation to work among this "older worker" group, but will not influence the earnings test for the midlife widows under consideration here ("Annual Statistical Supplement," 1986, Table B).

2

Background: Economics and the End of Marriage

ISSUES IN ECONOMIC ANALYSIS OF MARITAL TERMINATIONS

It may be taken as evidence of the relative inattention to the financial dimension of marital relationships that the majority of the research on transitions out of marriage focuses on the psychological and interpersonal dynamics, rather than on the economic consequences (Albrecht, Bahr, & Goodman, 1983; Glick, Weiss, & Parkes, 1974; Hunt, 1966; Kitson et al., 1985; Levinger, 1979; Lindemann, 1944; Lopata, 1973; Spanier & Furstenberg, 1982).

This chapter examines the evidence developed to date regarding the economic outcomes for women following the end of marriage in midlife. Material is divided into several major sections. The first examines changes in individual and household income following the termination of marriage, including variations by gender and other social traits. The second section examines information on how these changing income profiles translate into the risks of poverty following separation, widowhood, or divorce. A third section examines the research on the sources of income and their contributions in the households of formerly married women. The next section examines the labor force participation and change in employment activities among midlife women following marital termination. Another section discusses the connections between economic well-being and remarriage: What do we know regarding how each might affect the other?

The presentation focuses on the consequences for women, highlighting those specifically pertaining to midlife women; however, some comparative information on men is essential to an understanding of the divergent paths regarding income and poverty for the two sexes when marriage ends. These studies have used a variety of methodological approaches but seldom have compared divorced, separated, and widowed persons (for exceptions see Amato & Partridge, 1987; Morgan, 1990; Nestel, Mercier, & Shaw, 1983). The absence of substantial comparative research arises from two basic problems. First, it is difficult to collect adequate comparative data on women whose marriages end, because divorce (or separation) and widowhood occur at different average ages. Typical widows or divorcees are not only in different age ranges but are also members of different birth cohorts and lose their spouses during different stages of the family life cycle. These differences confound straightforward comparisons of marital transition consequences. Second, researchers have until quite recently been divided in their approach to the study of marital dissolution. Those specializing in gerontology and later-life families explored widowhood; those with a general family focus in sociology, psychology, and other social sciences examined divorce and its sequelae. This division of labor has largely precluded systematic attention to the central question of whether there are common consequences for financial well-being among women following separation, widowhood, or divorce.

Background of the Existing Research

With some notable exceptions (see, for example, Mallan, 1975), the research on the consequences of widowhood, divorce, and separation began by using income or financial distress as an explanatory factor in studies of psychological well-being or adaptation (Lopata, 1973; Morgan, 1976), and not as a central outcome or dependent variable of the analysis. Thus early studies considered the economic transition when women were widowed, divorced, or separated of secondary conceptual importance. More recently, however, studies focusing on the income and poverty consequences of widowhood, separation, and divorce have become more common and more sophisticated. The results, as we shall see, still leave some questions unanswered for midlife women.

Studies of the economic consequences of marital termination use three primary methodologies. The first is the cross-sectional study, which presents a "snapshot" of information on various marital status categories at a given time. Although cross-sectional research provides valuable information on the relative well-being of each marital status group, it cannot assess the impact and consequences of the marital transition, because there is no "before" measurement (Duncan & Hoffman, 1985a). The second type of analysis is the posttransitional study. Posttransitional research selects individuals who have experienced particular forms of marital dissolution and examines both prospectively and retrospectively how their lives have changed since that event. Although posttransitional studies provide some evidence of change after the end of marriage, they suffer from sampling problems and the uncertainties of retrospective information, often asking people to recall events and information from several years earlier (Hyman, 1983).

The third methodology is the longitudinal analysis, which follows a large number of individuals over time as they move through various life events, including transitions out of marriage (Duncan & Hoffman, 1985a). Longitudinal studies permit researchers to examine change from before to after a marital transition without the problems of posttransitional studies (Hyman, 1983). Although they are expensive to mount and often have difficulty from sample attrition, longitudinal data provide the best basis for carefully documenting changes in income or poverty rates associated with marital termination. Results from each type of analysis help to build our current picture of the economic consequences of widowhood, separation, and divorce for midlife women.

CHANGES IN INCOME

Cross-sectional data from the U.S. Bureau of the Census confirm that women whose marriages have ended are economically disadvantaged compared to their married age peers, having significantly lower median household income amounts (U.S. Bureau of the Census, 1986a). These results have also been replicated in the annual surveys of the National Opinion Research Center (NORC) during the 1970s (Hyman, 1983). Younger widows and divorcees were more relatively disadvantaged than their older counterparts in comparison to the married in these surveys, but women of all marital categories had diminishing income levels as age increased. These differences undoubtedly reflect both cohort variations in earnings and differences in government support programs by age and marital status. Cross-sectional work, such as Lopata's (1973) study of women widowed after the age of 50, confirms that the differences hold across age groups. She shows that widows have lower levels of household income than do married couples of comparable ages, and are also worse off compared to their own economic status prior to widowhood.

Previously married men also report lower household income levels than their married counterparts in cross-sectional studies (U.S. Bureau of the Census, 1986b). This is to be expected, given that men also lose the earnings and other resources provided by their wives when their marriages end. The correlates of the early end of marriage for poorer individuals through death, separation, or divorce (e.g., youthful marriage, less education) also operate for both men and women. Just as financially disadvantaged wives face greater odds of a marriage that is cut short, so, too, are disadvantaged men more likely to experience widowerhood or divorce. Because there are differences in remarriage behavior and mortality rates by sex, however, there are fewer males than females in the ranks of the separated, divorced, or widowed at any given time (U.S. Bureau of the Census, 1977).

How dramatic are the changes for men and women? One posttransitional study (Kim, Brehm, & Lopata, 1977) showed that incomes of women who had been widowed for various lengths of time were about half of what they had been prior to widowhood. Duncan and Hoffman's longitudinal comparisons (1985a) find divorced women to drop to 70% of their predivorce household income levels, and remain there barring remarriage. With the passage of time and the growth in income among the married unmatched by women who are divorced, incomes in divorced households may reach one half of what they might have been had the marriage endured (Weiss, 1984).

Pett and Vaughn-Cole (1986) showed that one third of the men in their sample reported increases in dollar value of household income following divorce, although one third of women reported a loss of more than $8,000.[1] Over 40% of divorcing households headed by women saw their incomes immediately cut by more than one half, while only one sixth of divorced or separated men experienced a comparable drop (Duncan & Hoffman, 1985a). A study of widowed individuals found that one year after the death of a spouse, men experienced no real decline in income, but women faced a significant drop, placing them at greater risk of extreme poverty (Zick & Smith, 1986). Another study verified an income loss among widowers, although it was not as sharp as that among widows (Hyman, 1983). Five years after the death of a spouse a decline in economic well-being was found for widowed individuals of both sexes (Zick & Smith, 1986). Yet because both sexes, and especially men, are widowed at ages beyond 60, the income decline may be related as much to retirement as widow(er)hood.

Race and class appear as important differentiating factors in the consequences reported by formerly married women in several longitudinal studies. Although black women are economically disadvantaged relative to their white counterparts during marriage, once the divorce process begins white women experience greater relative decline in economic standing, diminishing the prior differences between the two groups (Hoffman, 1977). In several analyses of divorce the decline in per capita or household income was greatest for women whose incomes had been highest during marriage and smaller for women from poorer couples (Duncan & Hoffman, 1985a; Mauldin, 1990; Weiss, 1984; Weitzman, 1985). The negative effects in other studies, however, appear to be most severe for those who had the lowest incomes during marriage, including black women (Duncan & Hoffman, 1985a; Pett & Vaughn-Cole, 1986). Black women, however, still experience significant income drops after leaving marriage, and are less likely than whites to "recover" through remarriage (Duncan & Hoffman, 1985a). This apparent discrepancy means that women who were economically advantaged have the most resources to lose when facing the end of marriage, but those who are already at risk of being poor, although seeing more modest income decreases, are none-theless more frequently pushed over the edge into poverty.

But absolute levels of household income only tell part of the story. Because households with women and dependent children require more resources than those containing a single adult of either gender, other studies have examined income relative to "needs," often established on the basis of the current U.S. poverty level for households of specific sizes and composi-tions (see Orshansky, 1968). Using such criteria, the research suggests that following divorce, the economic well-being of women declines while that of their former husbands improves (Duncan & Hoffman, 1985a; Hoffman, 1977; Hoffman & Duncan, 1988; Weitzman, 1985). Although absolute income levels for husbands may decline, their needs decline even further, creating an overall improvement in economic well-being (Hoffman, 1977).

There is disagreement, however, regarding the magnitude of these changes. Weitzman's (1985) analysis suggests that the women experience a 73% decline in their standard of living, although their husbands experience a 42% improvement in their economic well-being approximately one year after the final divorce decree. Another analysis, using the longitudinal Panel Study of Income Dynamics, found that the income-to-needs ratios of women fell substantially less, averaging a 30% decline in the first year of divorce. In another study the economic well-being (income compared to needs) of divorced men improved 17% over a 7-year span, while that of their former wives had declined by 29% from married levels (Kitson with Holmes, in press). This difference is explained by the limited financial responsibilities (i.e., child support) men had toward their children who were in the custody of their ex-wives. Most researchers conclude that the direction of change is as Weitzman describes, with women's income status declining and that of their former spouses improving, but that the true magnitude over time is smaller than Weitzman reports (Hoffman & Duncan, 1988). As a result of these less adequate income levels, an Australian study, comparing 21 widowed mothers with 21 divorced and 21 married mothers, found difficulty in affording necessities, regardless of whether death or divorce ended the marriage (Amato & Partridge, 1987).

Comparative longitudinal studies also confirm that these changes are not temporary or transitory. Longitudinal analyses for up to 10 years confirm that formerly married women experience decrements in income, which typically persist barring remarriage (Arendell, 1987; Duncan & Hoffman, 1985a; Hoffman & Holmes, 1976; Holden et al., 1986; Morgan, 1981; Smith & Zick, 1986; Weiss, 1984; Zick & Smith, 1986). One analysis, focusing on midlife women over a 7-year time period, showed severe, negative economic consequences following the ending of marriage. Money income dropped 40% over these years, and the ratio of household income to needs dropped by more than 10% (Corcoran, 1979). A second study on midlife women over 10 years (Nestel et al., 1983) reports that women who had not remarried had income levels 35%-40% below those before their marriages ended, whereas the continuously married reported a real increase in income of 30% during the 10 years. Nestel and his associates (1983) suggest that the loss in income among women experiencing widowhood or divorce was partially offset by reduction in household size due to child-launching during this same 10-year period. So although incomes declined dramatically, economic well-being decreased somewhat less. A third study, using demographic data to examine consequences of widowhood and divorce among women over 40, found significant negative effects on home ownership and a reduction in economic well-being. The divorced women were more likely to be employed and were judged to be more economically vulnerable than their widowed counterparts (Uhlenberg, Cooney, & Boyd, 1990).

Studies of the changes following the move to no-fault divorce confirm that economic factors other than income have also recently changed for women, including lower property settlement amounts, shorter time periods for alimony payments, and fewer women receiving substantial cash settlements upon divorce (McLindon, 1987). Thus the average divorced woman is further disadvantaged by the sale of the family home, made necessary in order to provide for an equal distribution of joint assets as required by many states (Weitzman, 1985).

THE RISKS OF POVERTY

The poverty rate, an income level established by the government specific to households of various sizes, locations, and compositions, serves as the basis for determining who is and is not poor in most research and policy applications (see Orshansky, 1968).[2] Risks of poverty are difficult to estimate overall because households move into and out of poverty over time. Thus only a subset of midlife women who might experience poverty following (or as a consequence of) termination of marriage will be poor at any given point in time.

In terms of poverty rates, as the cross-sectional data in Table 1.1 showed, the divorced and widowed fare somewhat better than the separated but have considerably higher levels of poverty at all ages than their married peers. Poverty, for the most part, has been shown to follow widowhood rather than precede it (Hyman, 1983). One longitudinal study found that a general sample of widowed persons had a 33% chance of falling into poverty during the first 5 years of widowed status (Smith & Zick, 1986). Older women who become widowed faced a 64% risk of falling into poverty at least once during a 10-year period (Holden et al., 1986). Although many poor widows escape poverty again, more than half of these once-poor widows fall below the poverty line again within the subsequent 6 years (Holden et al., 1986).

Although poverty rates increase for women who divorce, they fall slightly for divorced men (Duncan & Hoffman, 1985a). Duncan and Hoffman show an immediate post-divorce increase of 75% in poverty among women who remain unremarried for a least five years (1985a). Long-term recovery from poverty is only slight. Weiss (1984) notes that the divorced poor tend to remain poor, whereas the married poor have better chances of improving their lot. Ironically, the position of divorced women in poverty is constrained by the fact that they are likely to have poor ex-husbands, unable to contribute to the household via child support (Beller & Graham, 1985).

Overall, research focusing on midlife women reports that about 40% of widows and 26% of divorcees, excluding those who remarry, experience some episode of poverty during the first 5 years following termination of marriage (Morgan, 1990). An individual's age, gender, length of marriage, and prior labor force experience influence the odds of becoming poor after separation, widowhood, or divorce. Individuals who are older, have had longer marriages, and have more experience in the labor force are less likely to become poor (Morgan, 1990; Smith & Zick, 1986).

SOURCES OF INCOME

With the transition out of marriage a major source of household income derived from the husband's earnings, business profits, or pension diminishes or disappears. Other sources of income may enter into the picture to compensate partially for this loss, with their relative importance varying by socioeconomic status (Weiss, 1984). Income that is transferred from other sources (ex-husbands, pensions, insurance, or public coffers) into the households of formerly married women, however, varies both in amount and in the assumptions that underlie its award (Corcoran, 1979; Lopata & Brehm, 1986). In general these replacement sources of income do not provide a comparable standard of living to what the midlife woman (and her children) experienced prior to the end of marriage, and in some instances little new income is provided at all (Cherlin, 1981). Further detail regarding these replacement sources of income, their role in the overall composition of income following the end of marriage, and the assumptions underlying their award is provided below.

Divorced Women

Divorced individuals generally have significantly fewer sources of income shortly after marriage ends than those who remain married (Kitson with Holmes, in press). This gap in number of sources diminishes over time, however, and disappears in 2-3 years as the divorced group increases the number of sources from which they derive income.

One important source of income that is new for some divorcing women is earnings from employment. Divorced women as a group rely heavily on their earnings as a component of their total income, with the size of the contribution varying based on a number of factors such as age, education, prior work experience, and presence and ages of children (Kitson with Holmes, in press). The importance of earnings to overall income of divorced women is verified by studies revealing that those who are currently employed report the highest household incomes, but divorced women without earnings lag far behind in both total income and income adequacy (Weiss, 1984).

One comparative study of midlife women experiencing marital disruptions found that for white divorcees and widows the woman's earnings became a larger share of total income after the marriage ended, although this was not true for black women (Corcoran, 1979). This difference does not, however, imply an unwillingness or lack of participation in the labor force by black divorcees and widows. Instead, black women were limited in how much they could increase their earnings contribution to income because more of them had already been employed before their marriages ended (Corcoran, 1979).

A major contributing factor to economic distress among the divorced is nonpayment or incomplete payment of child support (Weiss, 1984). Data from the Census Bureau for 1985 show that 26% of women awarded child support received no payment, and only 48.2% received the full amount they were awarded (U.S. Bureau of the Census, 1987a). In another study, one quarter of the women reported receiving money from spouses for child support or alimony shortly after the divorce, but rates of payment improved over time (Kitson with Holmes, in press). Receipt of ordered child support is related to the traits of the ex-husband, improving as his income level increases (Beller & Graham, 1985). In both divorce and separation, characteristics of the woman, such as her education and earnings capacity, and those of her children (i.e., number and ages) also influence awards (Beller & Graham, 1985). The court-determined child support amount does not typically cover the costs of child-rearing, so that even if it is paid regularly and in full it is inadequate (Arendell, 1987; Gates, 1977). The difference must be provided by divorced mothers from other income sources or adjustments to family lifestyle.

Alimony, commonly thought to be an important source of income, has long been provided only to about 14%-15% of women, typically those with the longest marriages and with relatively wealthier spouses (Gates, 1977; U.S. Bureau of the Census, 1987a; Weitzman, 1985). Again, not all women who are awarded such support receive it. Only 73.3% of women awarded alimony or spousal support payments reported receipt of at least part of their awarded amount in 1985 (U.S. Bureau of the Census, 1987a). For the great majority of divorced women, then, alimony or spousal support is a source of income they see only in the movies. Those currently receiving spousal support are likely to have it as only a temporary benefit, on the assumption that they will "rehabilitate" themselves and be able to provide adequately for their own needs through employment after a few years (Weitzman, 1985).

Divorced women are five times more likely than their married peers to receive money from the welfare system (Kitson with Holmes, in press), a difference explained both by varying levels of need and by provisions in the systems of most states against supporting "intact" families. Black women relied more on transfers—Aid to Families with Dependent Children (AFDC), food stamps—to supplement postmarital income than did white women (Corcoran, 1979; Peterson, 1989), receiving nearly equal income contributions from alimony/child support and welfare programs in one study (Hoffman, 1977). Women divorced from previously low-income households continue to rely on governmental transfers (welfare) several years after the end of marriage, although households that were in the middle-income range prior to divorce are able to move more quickly away from reliance on public assistance (Weiss, 1984).

Widowed Women

For widows, benefits provided by the Social Security Administration are an important source of income. Lopata (1973) reports that 75% of respondents in her sample of widows more than age 50 reported that at least one member of their households received benefits from Social Security. These benefits constitute an average of 58% of household income (Lopata, 1979). Widowed mother benefits, provided by the Social Security system for women with dependent children, and support to offspring of deceased workers are also important sources of income to midlife widows with children (Lopata, 1979; Mallan, 1975; Morgan, 1981). Black women rely more on Social Security benefits than do white widows (Lopata, 1979).

As already mentioned, earnings are also a critical source of income in the households of widows (Lopata, 1973; Mallan, 1975). In one study of older widows, earnings provided a larger dollar amount to most households than did benefits from Social Security (Lopata, 1973). A sample of midlife widows (Morgan, 1981) showed that earnings gradually became a more important source of income with the passage of time, with about 30% of overall income to widowed households coming from earnings and another 30% from Social Security 3-4 years after death of spouse.

Among older widows, earnings from investments or savings were received by 30% of one sample (Lopata, 1973), but midlife widows have had less time to accumulate capital resources that might provide such income, making it a smaller component of income for them. Older widows also may rely heavily on public or private pension benefits, if their husbands selected a joint or survivor option in setting up pension benefits (Mallan, 1975; Miller, 1985). The Retirement Equity Act of 1985 now requires that survivor options providing continuing payment to a surviving spouse at the cost of lower monthly pension benefits be approved or rejected by both members of the couple (Miller, 1985). Although this may improve conditions for many future widows, the circumstances of the poorest elderly widows will be less affected, because they are less likely to have been married to men with private pensions.

ECONOMIC FACTORS AS A CAUSE
OF MARITAL TERMINATION

The causal relationship between the ending of marriage and financial disadvantage for women is far from clear. As we have seen, separation, widowhood, and divorce are positively associated with such disadvantage for women. Research evidence over the past several years also suggests that economic problems during marriage may contribute to marital termination (Albrecht, 1979). This is perhaps easiest to see in instances of divorce or separation. Couples fighting about money and those who are consistently stressed by inadequate financial resources may more often find themselves headed toward divorce (Albrecht, 1979). Research on the divorce rate confirms that couples with lower incomes are more likely to experience divorce or separation (Bahr, 1979; Mott & Moore, 1979). Although it is not clear whether economic distress is a cause or simply a coincidental factor, the notion must be entertained until proven otherwise that economic problems and poverty may serve as contributing factors to divorce and separation (Mott & Moore, 1979). Studies of income maintenance experiments suggest that increased income to wives has an independence effect, increasing divorce by diminishing reliance on their spouses. This effect was largest in poorer households in the study, however, and decreased as total household income levels increased (Hannan, Tuma & Groenveld, 1977, 1978).

Although the connection to widowhood does not appear initially to be as clear as that for divorce, women from economically distressed couples can anticipate being widowed at earlier ages than their counterparts with higher incomes. Long-established information on differential mortality shows that individuals from lower socioeconomic backgrounds are likely to die at younger ages than their more well-to-do counterparts (Kitigawa & Hauser, 1973). What is it about economic disadvantage that increases mortality? First, marginal income may mean that individuals eat less nutritious meals, live in more dangerous environments, and have less access to adequate health care. Second, poorer individuals may work at jobs that are physically riskier. Finally, the economic distress itself may contribute to stress, which aggravates health problems and may contribute to an earlier than otherwise anticipated death.

In longitudinal analyses of divorce (Duncan & Hoffman, 1985a; Kitson with Holmes, in press; Nestel et al., 1983; Peterson, 1989), however, the economic status of widowed or divorced individuals in the final year of marriage was shown to be lower than that of couples who would subsequently remain married. In other words, the couples in which divorce or widowhood occurred had lower household incomes than those that remained married, even during the marriage. Either financial distress contributes to marital termination, the declining income associated with marital transition has already begun within the final year of marriage, or other factors related to marital dissolution are also associated with economic status.

What all of this suggests, then, is that comparisons of income or poverty rates between married and divorced, separated, or widowed women must be done with caution. Although it is a simple strategy to compare these groups without additional comment, and to suggest that any disadvantage among those women outside marriage was due to their marital statuses, as is done in cross-sectional studies, such comparisons have added dimensions. Some financial disadvantages may precede and contribute to, while others may follow and derive from, marital termination. It becomes essential, therefore, to examine the characteristics of women both before and after their marriages end to ensure that attributions of cause for differences on economic indicators following the ending of marriage are not exaggerated or incorrectly made.

Pretransition Changes
in Economic Status

Comparison of pretransition status is especially important, since individuals may make financial, as well as other, preparations if they are aware that the end of their marriage is approaching (Fethke, 1984, 1989; Kitson with Holmes, in press; Roach & Kitson, 1989). In anticipation of their divorce, women may take charge of joint bank or investment accounts, enter the labor force, build a financial "nest egg," or supplement education or career training (Kitson with Holmes, in press; Peterson, 1989). Similarly, wives who know in advance about the impending deaths of their husbands may take preparatory steps in anticipation of that event (O'Bryant & Morgan, 1989). One comparative analysis found that women who divorced undertook more preparatory activities than did their counterparts who became widowed, a difference that may be partly due to age (Roach & Kitson, 1989).

Economic adjustments associated with the ending of marriage, then, may start even before steps are under way to end the marriage (in cases of divorce or separation) or well prior to the spouse's death (in the case of widowhood). The process of change associated with the end of marriage, then, extends not only after the fact, but may include activities prior to individuals being identified as widowed, separated, or divorced. The posttransition or longitudinal studies that have asked women to compare current conditions with those during their final year of marriage may inadvertently overlook such pretransition adjustments in the economic sphere. These preparatory changes argue for taking a longer-range view in order to gain a more complete understanding of the dynamics of the economic change as women move through the end of marriage.

LABOR FORCE PARTICIPATION AS AN ADAPTIVE STRATEGY

Both widowed and divorced women face financial and social pressures to seek employment or improve existing employment. For women not already employed, termination of marriage creates increased financial incentives to work for wages, so some newly widowed or divorced women do enter or return to work in response. The movement into the labor force may also be motivated by social identity or role considerations (Lopata, 1973), but income requirements are believed to be the most significant motivators.

Most studies suggest that increases in labor force participation among women follow marital termination of all types (Duncan & Hoffman, 1985a; Morgan, 1984; Peterson, 1989). Specifically, a study of divorcing women found that most who were homemakers moved into full-time employment within 2-3 years, and even those with full-time jobs frequently took on additional part-time work or additional hours of work (Kitson with Holmes, in press). Another longitudinal comparison found considerable increases in labor force participation for women experiencing widowhood, divorce, or separation during midlife (Nestel et al., 1983). White women make more labor force adjustments after marriages end, because more black women are already working full time (Corcoran, 1979).

Some studies on changes in labor force involvement, however, have shown fewer women entering or increasing involvement in jobs following marital transition than had been anticipated (Morgan, 1981, 1984; Weiss, 1984). One reason for these lower-than-expected rates of entry into jobs is that more and more women facing marital transitions are already employed. This means that the opportunity for adapting to the marital transition, either socially or financially, by going to work is increasingly limited (Morgan, 1980). Older women, more likely to be widowed than divorced, are less willing or interested in employment after their loss than younger widows because they were socialized to have more traditional expectations regarding gender and the employment of women (Morgan, 1981; Weitzman, 1985). Those women who have never worked and find themselves divorced or widowed in middle to later life encounter considerable difficulty in locating employment that will support them adequately, not to mention matching their lifestyle during marriage (Cherlin, 1981; Kitson with Holmes, in press; Pursell & Torrence, 1980). Given the earnings gap between men and women and the difficulties encountered by older or less experienced women in seeking employment, it is not surprising that finding jobs to provide adequate wages continues to be a problem for women who have recently faced the end of marriage (Bielby & Baron, 1986; Pursell & Torrence, 1980; Snyder, Miller, Hollenshead & Ketchin, 1984) .

Younger and midlife women are more likely to face other difficulties— in finding adequate and affordable child care to enable them to work (Mallan, 1975; Sidel, 1986). The lack of affordable child care means that some women with children will choose to remain dependent on government transfer programs such as AFDC or Social Security, because there is little apparent income advantage in taking a job (Berch, 1982; Sidel, 1986). This can further reduce long-range employment prospects for women and limit overall earnings and pension benefits for the future (O'Rand & Landerman, 1984; VanVelsor & O'Rand, 1984). As discussed earlier, widowed mothers receiving benefits from Social Security face an earnings test (Lopata & Brehm, 1986; Mallan, 1975). The effect of this test is to marginally reduce the attractiveness of employment.

REMARRIAGE AND ECONOMIC WELL-BEING

Researchers know relatively little about the motivations of individuals who seek remarriage, but have developed some interesting hypotheses and suggestive information on the categories of women who are more or less likely to remarry. Recent research suggests that the probability of remarriage, like that of marital termination, is influenced not only by age and gender, but also by income level (Day & Bahr, 1986; Uhlenberg et al., 1990; U.S. Bureau of the Census, 1977).

The economic theory of marriage suggests that women who have been the most financially dependent on kin or spouse and the most attractive as potential partners are most likely to remarry (Becker et al., 1976; Cherlin, 1981). This suggests that remarriage serves as an avenue of escape from poverty for women with limited alternatives (Albrecht et al., 1983). If marriages are formulated in order to resolve poverty or problems of limited income, the potential for their success as interpersonal relationships fulfilling our cultural and personal expectations is compromised. Further, economically motivated remarriage suggests that the institution is perceived by some women as the only means of assuring themselves an adequate lifestyle. Findings showing that women turn to remarriage only when they are unable to provide for themselves and their children define the institution as coercive rather than voluntary, and fly in the face of our stated values regarding the purpose of marriage.

Recent studies show that remarriage following divorce is becoming somewhat less common for women, down from 75% to approximately 70% (Norton & Moorman, 1987). This decrease has been tied to a variety of factors, prominently including the increased labor force activity and earnings of women. Further, analyses of census data show that the time interval between the end of a first marriage in divorce and initiation of a second is increasing, to approximately 1.5 years on the average (Norton & Moorman, 1987). The researchers analyzing these data conclude that perhaps the pattern of moving to a legal dissolution in order to be free to formalize a new relationship through remarriage is becoming less common, and instead that more individuals are terminating marriages without a new marital prospect waiting in the wings.

Remarriage rates and timing vary according to several factors. It is well known that men are more likely than women to remarry following the termination of marriage (Cherlin, 1981). Being currently employed increases the odds of remarriage for women, perhaps through providing access to new potential partners (Peters, 1986). With advancing age the likelihood of remarriage lessens for both genders but especially for women (Glick & Lin, 1986; Guttentag & Secord, 1983; Treas & VanHilst, 1976; Uhlenberg et al., 1990). Midlife and older women have more difficulty remarrying because of the higher mortality rates of males, resulting in fewer male than female survivors as age increases. Given these age differences, it is not surprising to learn that widows in Lopata's (1979) study who remarried were somewhat younger at widowhood and more educated than their non-remarrying counterparts. In addition there may be attitudinal barriers to remarriage, as found by Lopata (1979), among widows who had nursed their husbands during a final illness and did not wish to repeat the experience. Interestingly, the remarriers in that widowed sample also appear to have been more affluent in their earlier marriages than widows who did not remarry. When asked in an open-ended format to list the advantages of remarriage, 16% of the remarried widows volunteered financial advantages (Lopata, 1979).

Several other factors have been associated with the probabilities of remarriage. First, earlier studies had shown that the presence of children, especially in large numbers, discouraged remarriage, but this idea has not been supported by recent research. Glick and Lin (1986) suggest that childless divorced women have greater potential to remain unmarried, surviving independently on their own earnings without the expense of child care. Recent research shows that children may lengthen the time to remarriage (Peters, 1986), but the deterrent effect of children on remarriage is no longer a strong deterrent (Glick & Lin, 1986).

Both education and employment experience have been found to have somewhat contradictory effects in previous studies on the remarriage of women. Greater education and work experience appear to reduce the odds of remarriage for women by enabling them to earn sufficient income to live independently (Glick & Lin, 1986; Peters, 1986). Remarriages among poorer women are more frequent according to Glick & Lin (1987), because women were seeking a man who would be able to support them and their children. Other factors including race, foreign birth, and time since marriage ended have been shown to shape the odds of remarriage for widows, divorcees, or both (Nestel et al., 1983), or to influence the timing of remarriage (Peters, 1986).

Divorced women in one study who were identified as wanting to remarry for monetary reasons were less satisfied with their lives than were those seeking remarriage for other reasons (Spanier & Thompson, 1984). Another analysis of divorced white women showed them to be upwardly mobile in remarriage, with most selecting second husbands with more education and a higher status occupation than their first partners (Mueller & Pope, 1980).

An in-depth interview study found that women who were poor accepted dates with men they characterized as undesirable in the hope of finding a marriage partner, and were more interested in remarriage than other women in the sample (Ambert, 1983). Another investigation of divorce (Kitson with Holmes, in press) showed that divorced women with fewer resources were more likely to remarry, although the opposite was true for men. The researchers conclude that women seek partners to improve their income situation, while men in poorer financial circumstances are less able to attract new wives. Confirmation for this argument comes from two studies. The first finds that divorced women awarded alimony or child support are less likely to remarry than other divorcees (Beller & Graham, 1985). Analysis of a panel study of low-income women also found that those not receiving welfare support were three times as likely to remarry following divorce than their welfare recipient peers, but that this pattern held only among whites (Bahr, 1979).

Relatively little research has systematically examined the income or poverty consequences when women do remarry. Presumably the relative benefits would vary according to race, education, and a variety of other determinants of the new husband's earnings (Duncan & Hoffman, 1985a). Older widows who remarried were, not surprisingly, better off economically after remarriage than widows who remained single (Lopata, 1979). Five years after divorce average income for remarried divorcees exceeded pre-divorce level, either because of the natural earnings increase with advancing age or selection of higher earning husbands for subsequent marriages (Duncan & Hoffman, 1985b).

DIFFERENCES: DIVORCED, WIDOWED, AND SEPARATED WOMEN

The odds of experiencing divorce and widowhood are not randomly distributed in the population, but vary along some clearly defined dimensions. Many of these dimensions have come to be "common knowledge" among those who study the family (Glenn & Supancic, 1984). We have already discussed some of the ways in which age is associated with widowhood and divorce and the difficulties involved in separating out the effects of age and cohort membership from those due to marital status. Age at marriage is also significantly associated with the probability of divorcing (Glenn & Supancic, 1984). Research also shows that divorce rates have been increasing for women over 40, so later-life divorce will become a more important focus in the future (Uhlenberg et al., 1990).

The presence of children has a dampening effect on the rate of divorce, with childless couples experiencing higher rates of marital dissolution (U.S. Bureau of the Census, 1977). The odds of divorce are higher for second or subsequent marriages, suggesting that those who have once divorced are also more amenable to resolving an unhappy second marriage through legal dissolution (Furstenberg & Spanier, 1984). In addition, a variety of other sociodemographic characteristics have been shown to be related to the probability of divorce. Data from the U.S. Census show that black couples have higher risks of divorce than do white couples, and that couples with more educated and higher earning husbands have lower rates of divorce. In couples in which the wives have more than 5 years of education beyond high school the probability of divorce is higher than among those in which wives have lower educational attainment (Norton & Moorman, 1987; U.S. Bureau of the Census, 1977). Higher earnings of the wife may also reflect attitude differences from their less educated peers (Cherlin, 1979; Ross & Sawhill, 1975). There is even evidence that the probability of divorce may be transmitted intergenerationally (Pope & Mueller, 1979), or that living in the "divorce belt" (regions of the country with higher than average divorce rates) increases the odds of legal termination of marriage (Glenn & Supancic, 1984).

Little mention has been made in this review of the literature regarding the separated, because the information on them as a group is much more fragmentary. The separated are a unique category, because their marriages are neither operating nor fully terminated. Research shows that separated women are less likely to be awarded child support or alimony (Beller & Graham, 1985), are less likely to work, have lower incomes, and are more commonly members of racial minorities (Peterson, 1989). Cherlin (1981) found large numbers of separated women whose disadvantaged economic status he interpreted as preventing them from affording the legal costs of a divorce. In general, however, little specific research attention has been paid to the separated, who are often considered to be nothing more than women in transition between marriage and divorce.

Becoming widowed is related to age more than any other variable, because in this case the marriage is not ended voluntarily. Mortality rates are themselves related to social and demographic traits (Kitigawa & Hauser, 1973). Those widowed in midlife are disproportionately likely to be poor, less educated, and members of racial minorities. As age increases and mortality becomes less selective, widows become more representative of the female population at large (Kitigawa & Hauser, 1973).

Some of the selection factors for widowhood and divorce in midlife are similar. The nonrandom processes selecting individuals into widowed, separated, and divorced status also suggest that women who are to become formerly married are from less advantaged socioeconomic backgrounds and differ, long before their marriages end, from their counterparts who will remain married (Morgan, 1979; Burkhauser, Holden, & Myers, 1986; Peterson, 1989).

SUMMARY AND CONCLUSIONS

Examination of the research of all types that has been performed to date suggests several major conclusions. First, women experiencing the ending of their marriages, regardless of the means by which they end, typically experience declines in economic well-being. This decline does not occur equally for men nor are all women equally affected. In the case of divorce, the women who lose the most are those who had the highest incomes during marriage, typically incomes that relied heavily on high earnings of their husbands. Race, age, education, employment, and family status also appear to influence the economic fortunes of women as they move from married to formerly married. For example, midlife women lacking prior work experience or with young or numerous children are constrained in the extent to which employment can provide a remedy for any economic problems following termination of marriage.

Some important parallels appear in the effects of the end of marriage on divorced, widowed, and separated women, although the information on separation is sparse. All women experience overall declines in economic well-being and become more reliant on their own earnings and public transfers for their support. Major differences appear in the sources of income provided to widowed and divorced/separated households. Households of divorced women depend more on income transferred from the ex-husband, who generally continues to earn income, which he may be legally required to share through child or spousal support. Widows, on the other hand, seldom have resources other than insurance or occasional pension benefits from their late husbands, and must rely on benefits from Social Security in addition to their own earnings.

There remain some questions and problems in drawing conclusions from these analyses regarding the overall impact of the end of marriage on economic status of midlife women. First and foremost, few studies are comparative. Studies done on different samples and with diverse research techniques often provide contradictory or inconsistent results that are difficult to reconcile. They leave questions regarding whether differences are real or artifacts of the way in which data were collected or analyzed. Second, several of the longitudinal studies do not actually follow individuals all of the way through the processes of separation, widowhood, or divorce. Instead, even a longitudinal analysis may examine the final year of marriage and the circumstances of the widow or divorcee 5-7 years after the fact. Few studies follow women repeatedly over time as they move into the ranks of the formerly married. This leaves us with several unanswered questions. Does the separation, widowhood or divorce create an immediate and long-term change in income assets or risks of poverty? Does economic well-being erode slowly over time? Are there fluctuations in economic status as individuals recover from the disruption coincident with the end of marriage? Do some people go into poverty and quickly escape again before they are counted in cross-sectional studies? Unfortunately, few studies to date provide this type of detail. Finally, most of the longitudinal analysis available is based on one study, the Panel Study of Income Dynamics (Corcoran et al., 1984; Duncan & Hoffman, 1985a; Hoffman, 1977; Hoffman & Holmes, 1976; Myers, Burkhauser & Holden, 1987; Smith & Zick, 1986). This study, which began with 5,000 American families, followed them over time as individuals married, had children, and were divorced or widowed, with an eye to their economic fortunes. Although this is a large and reputable study, over reliance on any one study for conclusions risks validity. Use of multiple sources of data enhances the credibility of findings.

As we have seen, it is not sufficient simply to examine economic profiles or the rates of poverty either immediately after a marital transition (Hyman, 1983; Peterson, 1989) or at one subsequent point in time to get a true picture of the economic risks of the ending of marriage. In the analysis that follows, women will be tracked over the course of several years after their marriages end, documenting the overall financial outcomes and comparing the relative well-being of divorced, widowed, and separated women in midlife.

The analysis uses a prominent longitudinal data set, the National Longitudinal Surveys (NLS) cohort of mature women. These data are described in much greater detail elsewhere (Center for Human Resource Research, 1983; Shaw, 1983; Sproat, Churchill, & Sheets, 1985). An original sample of 5,083 women between the ages of 30-44 were interviewed between 1967 and 1982. By the end of this 15-year period they ranged in age from 45-59. Data are available for each woman detailing her marital status and family characteristics, employment, health, income, and numerous additional variables of interest. The next chapter provides a more detailed description of the data and characteristics of the women in their marriages as a baseline.

NOTES

1. Increases in incomes for men over time is not surprising, given typical raises and cost of living increases. It is, however, also possible that men increase their involvement in the labor force by working more hours, thereby increasing their levels of income. Research has documented such increasing labor force involvement for women (see material included in the section on labor force participation in this chapter), but has not specifically addressed this issue for formerly married men.

2. In some contemporary studies, researchers interested in greater flexibility also utilize categories of "near poor," typically those within 125%-150% of the poverty level. These individuals are considered to be experiencing economic hardship and are, in the judgment of many, justifiably included in discussions of poverty (Morgan, 1990).

3

Profile:
The NLS Sample
and Pretransition Traits

In order to proceed with the comparisons of economic fates of widowed, divorced, and separated women, it is essential to understand the nature of the information serving as the basis for addressing the research questions. It is also critical, as discussed earlier, to establish the economic and social status of the midlife women during marriage, prior to any changes deriving from divorce, widowhood, or separation. The first section of this chapter outlines the background of the study on midlife women and the methodological approach used to address the research questions posed in Chapter 1. A second major section compares the traits of the women during marriage, categorizing them according to whether they would remain married or face widowhood, separation, or divorce. That section examines the extent to which the social and economic characteristics varied across groups *before* their marriages ended. It also provides essential clues on related traits that must be examined in subsequent analyses in order to better distinguish the effects of leaving marriage from nonrandom selectivity.

METHODOLOGY OF THE STUDY

Sample Characteristics

The data employed throughout this analysis are drawn from the National Longitudinal Surveys cohort of mature women, from 1967-1982. The NLS studies have had as their central concern the labor force activity among various age/sex groups in the population. This particular panel study of midlife women, which was conceived in large measure to focus on returns to work of women who were completing childbearing, included an initial sample of 5,083 women between the ages of 30 and 44 years in 1967. During the 15-year span under consideration here, respondents were interviewed 11 times (yearly from 1967 to 1982, with the exceptions of 1970, 1973, and 1977). In-person interviews (6 times) alternated with telephone interviews. The very brief mail survey in 1968 gathered limited information that is not analyzed here. All interviews were conducted by staff from the U.S. Bureau of the Census (for further details see Center for Human Resource Research, 1983). Others have used these data to examine a variety of issues on midlife women from childbearing to employment, health, and retirement decisions (see Sproat et al., 1985).

Because the NLS panel study oversampled black women (at 3-4 times the sampling rates for whites) (Center for Human Resource Research, 1983), separate analyses by race will be a common feature in many of the figures and tables that follow. Without making the distinction by race, the estimates on some traits under examination, for example poverty and economic well-being, could be biased by the unusually high number of black respondents (e.g., inflating poverty rates over what they would be in a more racially representative sample). Such biases could also disproportionately influence specific groups, such as the separated, who in prior research have had higher percentages of black women in their ranks than is found in other marital status categories. For instance, if the separated have lower family incomes it would be impossible to determine whether this was due to marital status or racial composition unless such comparisons are performed. In the analyses that do not make distinctions by race, caution must be used in interpreting the results or attempting to generalize them to the larger population because of this oversampling of black women.[1]

The interview schedules used in the NLS study included considerable detail on the women's current employment and work history, health, marital status, family characteristics, and income. The income questions solicited detailed information regarding sources and amounts of income for various members of the household.[2] Except for 1968, respondents were asked in each interview to report their current marital status. In two years (1977 and 1982), retrospective marital history information was also gathered, which helped to validate the events reported in the year-by-year interviewing.

Using Longitudinal Surveys

Longitudinal studies such as the NLS mature women's cohort provide a wealth of useful data on the progression of events in peoples' lives.

Studies that include such repeated measurements provide the opportunity to observe changes happening to individuals in a naturalistic fashion, as some of them move through major life transitions such as the birth of a child or the loss of a spouse, or incremental changes simply occurring with the passage of time (Hyman, 1983). Longitudinal data thus provide real pre/post event measurement opportunities not possible in studies that select individuals after a particular transition such as divorce has taken place. And because repeated measurements enable the researcher to establish the time ordering of events, testing of causal hypotheses is sometimes possible. With proper controls for historical events (e.g., wars, recessions, unusually large birth cohorts) that may modify responses, it generates a form of quasi-experimental comparisons unavailable in many other contexts. In this analysis there is the opportunity to observe real changes in the circumstances of midlife women as they move from the economic protection of marriage to whatever financial and social outcomes await them in their postmarital lives.

Although longitudinal research is a valuable methodology, it also generates some special challenges for researchers. First, while the study is ongoing, research techniques improve and experience teaches how better to ask questions and organize data. Longitudinal researchers are, therefore, constantly tempted to change (and improve) their questions in subsequent surveys. The problem with implementing such improvements, however, is that they reduce comparability from one data collection to another, partially defeating the purpose of longitudinal study. A few such problems of data comparability were encountered in the NLS Mature Women's Cohort, including questions on income and on children in the household. Every effort has been made, through recoding and combining variables, to provide consistent information across time. When there are minor exceptions to this comparability, they are noted.

The second issue is attrition. In a lengthy and involved study such as this, respondents may decide to discontinue their participation after a time, or be lost through relocation, death, or other life disruptions. The NLS study through 1982 had a helpfully low rate of overall attrition, losing less than a third (30.3%) of its participants and maintaining a significant core group of respondents.

Given the focus of examination here, there is another form of sample change that is of concern. That is, individuals leave the widowed, separated, and divorced groups through a subsequent change in marital status. For the widowed and divorced this is through remarriage, although for the separated it may be either a subsequent divorce or a reconciliation.[3] Over time, as individuals leave the ranks of these groups, the multiple respondent base for estimating long-term effects shrinks. The real concern here is not simply the constraints of a smaller sample size, but rather the potential for such shrinkage to be selective, disproportionately involving women with a set of similar characteristics. For example, if women who remarry are more economically advantaged than their divorced peers who do not, we might erroneously conclude from examining the data that over time there is ongoing deterioration in income levels among midlife divorced women. This change over time would be a statistical artifact rather than a reality. Although this apparent deterioration was not *caused by* increasing time spent in divorce and individual women may not see their financial situations erode over time, it would nonetheless be a valid and potentially important finding that, as time goes on, the average incomes of those remaining divorced are lower. Put another way, if we know that the subgroup of women who leave marriage and remain unmarried have poorer economic prospects than those who remarry, the result would be of significance to research and policy. Conclusions must be drawn carefully, based on comparisons of women with their own prior status rather than the shifting status of the group as membership changes.

Selection of the Sample

Because the focus of attention here is on an examination of the consequences of transitions out of marriage via widowhood, separation, or divorce, only those women who listed themselves as married either with "spouse present" or "spouse absent" in 1967 were included in the study. The very small number of "married, spouse absent" respondents were retained, because their status undoubtedly varies from a brief separation for military service to hospitalization. Those listing themselves as "separated" in 1967, however, were excluded, because it was impossible to determine what their circumstances had been before their marriages were suspended.

The above restriction removed a large number of respondents in the original NLS panel from consideration ($N = 1,019$), including those divorced, widowed, or never married as of the 1967 interview. A second group of excluded respondents were those who withdrew from the study following the initial 1967 interview ($N = 230$). In these cases it was impossible to determine whether any marital status change ever occurred during the subsequent years. Because only a small group of women of races other than white or black was sampled, they were also excluded ($N = 69$). An additional few respondents ($N = 9$) were omitted from the sample because of unresolvable inconsistencies in their marital histories during the panel (1967-1982). The resulting pool of respondents in 1967 contained 3,756 women, or 73.9% of the original sample. These were the women for whom marital histories were constructed and who serve as the sample base for the analyses that follow.

Dealing with marital status over time

Establishing marital status and its changes was a critical task in preparing to answer the research questions. Although the task might appear straightforward, this turned out to be far from the case. The NLS information on marital status derives from the self-reports of the women in the study. It is assumed that their reports are, in the vast majority of cases, accurate representations of their marital and legal situations at the times they were interviewed. Marital transitions could only be identified consistently by a change in the reported marital status from one interview to the next. Individuals were counted as having a marital transition if there was a change from one marital status to another (e.g., from married to widowed) in two contiguous data points. One exception to this rule was the few instances in which an individual was missing for one or more interviews and then returned to the panel. In those cases the transition was reported as having occurred in the year of the respondent's return to the sample, barring contradictory evidence.

These detailed marital history questions, available in 1977 and 1982, were used whenever possible to verify the interview-by-interview information and to clarify response patterns that did not initially seem to make sense. In many cases it was difficult, even using this retrospective information, to pinpoint the month or year of the transition precisely.

Some midlife women move through transitions that at first appear to be impossible (e.g., from widowed to divorced, or from separated to married). Because there are in many cases two-year intervals between data collection points, some of the responses that initially appear illogical are correct. For example, a woman could divorce one spouse, marry another, and become widowed, with all of this occurring in a two-year span between interviews. Cases presenting such confusing information were individually examined, using the marital history questions available in 1977 and 1982. The responses showed that many of these seemingly illogical patterns were, in fact, correct versions of the marital histories of a few women. A few others apparently represent miscodes or misstatements by respondents.

Only a small number ($N = 9$) of NLS women whose marital histories were deemed impossible (e.g., married for seven interviews, and then reporting oneself as never married for four more) or undecipherable finally had to be excluded from the study. Once it became clear that individual marital histories could include more than one type of marital transition for a single individual (e.g., being both divorced and widowed during the 15 years, or being divorced, remarried, and again divorced), the matter of determining which transitions to examine came to the forefront. If only one type of transition was examined for each respondent, it would seriously reduce the number of women in each marital category, especially for the separated and divorced. In addition it could compromise the degree to which results represent the experience of midlife women. Therefore, the first instance each where a given respondent moves from marriage to widowhood, separation, or divorce or from formerly married to remarried is included. Thus it is quite possible for a midlife NLS woman to become divorced, to remarry, and to subsequently be widowed and have each of those three events included in the analyses.

For the majority of respondents experiencing any change only one transition is examined (71.5%), but for a few women more complex marital histories were the reality. About 5% of women with any marital status change reported three or all four of the possible transitions (including remarriage) had occurred to them during the 15-year period. The most complex marital sequence discovered was that of a woman who was married in 1967 and subsequently separated, reconciled with her husband, again separated, divorced, remarried, and finally widowed. It is important too, in terms of having results that are more reflective of the larger population, to include women such as those who follow a rather typical path including being separated, divorced, and then remarried.

The exception to this clear pattern of establishing transitions as movement from marriage to a formerly married state is among the divorced, where a significant number of women ($N = 105$, or 33.3% of the divorcing women) move from marriage to a recorded period of separation followed by divorce. These women are included in the separated category for the time they remain in that status, having entered from marriage, and are subsequently numbered among the divorced. Because these divorced women are a somewhat different class, moving into that status after passing through the ranks of the separated, some distinct analyses are performed to examine when the major changes occur for them relative to the stages of their marital dissolution. It is anticipated that they will show less change upon becoming divorced, because they had already had major adaptations in their lives and circumstances at the point of separation.

To structure the data on marital histories, four variables were created to indicate transition points, representing widowhood, divorce, separation, and remarriage. The codes for each of these variables reflect the time interval when the transition in question occurred (e.g., divorced 1979-1981, or remarried 1981-1982). In this fashion, each individual's set of marital transitions were coded to include both their type and timing. Individuals not experiencing a particular transition are coded with a zero for that variable, so that the women who remained married to the same spouse throughout the study scored zeros on all four of these marital transition variables. Due to the complexities of data management and their relatively small numbers, it was decided to omit consideration of second or third transitions of the same type that happen to a particular individual.

Issues for marital separation

In defining the separated, any women interviewed during a period of separation, regardless of how it ended (i.e., in divorce, reconciliation, or continuing separation), was included among the ranks of the separated. The number of separations enumerated in this study undoubtedly underestimates the total number that occurred over this 15-year span, because many of the briefer separations occurred between interviews (Morgan, 1988). Thus the NLS overrepresents those who had relatively long separations and so were "captured" by the interviewing process. Separations are conceptually difficult, because there is generally some level of change in the interpersonal and economic/legal aspects of the relationship. Legally the couple remains married, but in many senses, quite possibly including the economic aspects, the marital relationship is suspended or terminated. The amount of change in the relationship may, however, not be as clear-cut as in the cases of movement directly from marriage to divorce or widowhood. For example, the extent to which the income support from husbands is withdrawn remains unclear. Husbands may or may not help to support their wives and children, depending in part on the legal and interpersonal status of the relationship as well as the intended outcome of the separation. If the separation is viewed as a prelude to divorce, the change in the relationship on all levels, including the economic one, may be greater than if the outcome of the separation is uncertain. Therefore, the amount of change at separation in both social and economic dimensions of the marriage may vary widely across couples. The relatively high rate of reconciliation (Kitson & Langlie, 1984) suggests that the transition at separation is neither as complete nor as final as that occurring upon divorce.

There is one additional conceptual problem with respondents who are separated and who subsequently undergo a divorce. The question revolves around when the end of their marriage could actually be said to have occurred. Does it occur when one or both partners decide to end the ongoing marriage, when that decision takes the form of a residential separation, or at some specific point in the legal process of divorce? Researchers have treated separation in varying ways, with some including it with divorce as though the two transitions were equivalent (Peterson, 1989; Weiss, 1984). Others (Kitson, 1985) have selected the date of filing for divorce as the critical moment. Examination of responses to the retrospective questions in 1977 and 1982 suggests that the NLS respondents themselves disagreed on this point, with some identifying the end of their marriage at the time of separation, although others listed their marriage ending when the divorce took place. Although for some marital separation serves as a stepping stone to divorce, it is not universally so. Some respondents experience long periods of separation during the study, without either divorce or reconciliation by 1982, while others drop out of the panel before their separation is resolved (Morgan, 1988). Therefore, in this analysis separation is dealt with as a distinct form of marital termination.

Dealing with Time

Because the data collections did not occur at even time intervals, there are some complicating factors in analysis. For example, a woman divorcing between 1967 and 1969 (the first two full interviews) would have her first postdivorce interview somewhere between a few months to nearly two years after the divorce, the second up to four years after, and the third approximately five years after divorce. A woman divorcing between 1971 and 1972, however, would have her first interview within one year after the divorce, the second interview within three years, and the third interview five years into divorce. In essence, the timing of the interviews means that there is some lack of precision in comparing individuals at their first and second interviews after the marriage ends. Conveniently, regardless of what year the marriage ends, the third measurement point is approximately five years after marital transition. So throughout the analysis that follows, interview one is 1-2 years after transition, interview two is 3-4 years posttransition, the third interview is five years, and the fourth is 6-7 years after the marriage ends, and so on.

Marital transitions occurred at varying points in chronological time throughout the 15-year span covered in this analysis. Attempting to draw comparisons on individuals separated, widowed, and divorced at each time interval would provide very small comparison groups, making statistical analysis impractical. To avoid these difficulties and to deal more productively with the resource provided by a longitudinal study, synthetic cohorts were constructed (Campbell & Hudson, 1984). A synthetic cohort collects individuals experiencing a specific event—here transitions out of marriage—at different times and clusters them together for analysis. Using a synthetic cohort approach increases the sample size and statistical power of comparisons. For example, all individuals who were widowed at any point in the study were collected and handled as though they had all lost their spouses at the same hypothetical time in terms of the prewidowhood and postwidowhood comparisons.

This synthetic cohort strategy has two side effects. First, the researcher must attempt to control for any historical or temporal differences that might influence the process being studied. Of course, of central concern were changes in economic indicators over the time of the study due to inflation, aging of respondents, and modifications in labor force participation of women. By converting all income and asset amounts to 1981 equivalent dollars using the Consumer Price Index, effects of inflation were largely removed. Income amounts could then be compared in constant dollars, so that the timing of marital transition becomes less important. To reduce the effects of age and the passage of time, the married comparison group respondents were randomly assigned a Time0, theoretically comparable to the last interview prior to the end of marriage. This strategy helps to randomize any effects of other temporal trends on the married women, who serve as a basis for comparison with their age peers who became separated, divorced, or widowed.

Second, synthetic cohorts result in variable amounts of pre- and posttransition information. The sample was constructed so that each in- dividual would have at least one pretransition interview to serve as a baseline for comparison. However, midlife women who were widowed late in the panel, 1979 for example, would have had seven data collections prior to being widowed, and only two interviews after that change. In effect, the study design limits the amount of information on postmarital changes that can be gained from individuals whose marriages ended later in the survey. This also serves to reduce the numbers of individuals for whom long-term consequences can be estimated, but without introducing the serious potential for bias introduced by attrition.

On the positive side, the synthetic cohort strategy provides the opportunity to amass relatively large numbers of widowed, separated, and divorced women for comparative purposes, a feat unmatched in research on this topic to date. Given the fact that the NLS panel followed a large number of women over time, asking them the same questions repeatedly, synthetic cohorts allow a relatively unencumbered comparison of the changes occurring to separated, divorced, and widowed women with responses that are truly comparable.

Data Analyses

A rich resource, like a longitudinal study of this type, provides a body of information that can be analyzed in a variety of ways. The goal here is to outline in some detail the short and longer range changes in economic status following the end of marriage, and to examine how these changes influence other major life decisions having to do with labor force participation and remarriage. With that goal in mind, the analyses focus primarily on descriptive information. Comparisons include the critical factor of time and examine the diversity created by race, family configuration, education, prior economic status, and age in the outcomes of women as they move from marriage to one of the formerly married statuses.

Because many of the potential explanatory factors in outcomes experienced by formerly married women are interrelated, selective evaluations of their relative importance are made using appropriate multivariate techniques (OLS Regression, logistic regression) in future chapters. Results are limited to description of the relative importance of significant predictors. Because temporal ordering is apparent for only some of the variables, however, the extent to which causal conclusions can be drawn is limited.

PROFILE OF THE NLS SAMPLE

Just who are the women who experience widowhood, divorce, or separation, and how do they differ in the aggregate from each other and from women who remain married? In this section selected sociodemographic characteristics of women are examined and compared in the years before their marriages end. In some cases the data are from 1967, because certain traits were evaluated only at widely spaced intervals during the study and others (e.g., educational attainment) changed very little over time. Most characteristics are evaluated in the final interview prior to the marital transition (hereafter referred to as Time0). Because the closest pretransition interview might capture some of the early adaptations to changing marital status, as described in Chapter 2, checks are made against the prior interview (Time–1) when available, to determine whether such pretransition adaptations have taken place.

The characteristics compared are important variables that have appeared in the literature as differentiating among the marital groups. These comparisons provide baseline information on how the midlife women differ from one another even before any consequences of separation, widowhood, and divorce appear. Thus any differences seen here address the selectivity problem described earlier—that women with substantially different income levels and social traits are more likely to be "selected" into or spend a long period in formerly married statuses.

The results are also informative regarding the degree to which this sample represents the larger population from which it is drawn. If substantial differences are discovered between the NLS data and available census reports, they would suggest the need for caution in applying results drawn from this sample to the larger population. Parallels with existing information, on the other hand, increase confidence that the NLS women are representative of women nationally at similar ages and under comparable circumstances as they experience these transitions. As comparisons are drawn among women based on their prospective (future) marital status transitions, women will be referred to in terms of their future marital statuses; as married, widowed, divorced, and separated, in order to simplify the terminology. Although the names indicate known future transitions, it must be remembered that the comparisons in this chapter are based on data from interviews when all of the women were still married.

Frequency and Timing
of Marital Transitions

The first issue for consideration is the number of women who experience specific types of marital transitions, and when those transitions occur. The first table (Table 3.1) lists the frequencies of first separations, widowhoods, and divorces over the entire span of the study by five-year time intervals and by race. These events are also converted into average per year rates, based on the number of women starting each interval in marriage (thus at risk of having marital termination).

During the 15-year span, starting from a base of 3,756 married women, there were 349 instances of widowhood, 315 reported divorces, and 292 separations. Note that these are events, not individuals. It would be incorrect to add up the first column in Table 3.1 and conclude that marital termination affected over a quarter (25.4%) of the women who started this panel in marriages, because a few of the marital events reported in Table 3.1 are second or even third transitions occurring to single individuals. Only 22.3% of NLS women in marriages in 1967 had experienced at least one transition out of marriage by 1982.

Table 3.1 Number of Marriages Ending by Type of Termination, Race, and Time Interval

| | *Total Events (Rates)* [a] | *5-Year Intervals* | | |
		1967-1972	*1972-1977*	*1977-1982*
Widowed	349	100	113	136
	(6.2)	(5.3)	(6.9)	(10.0)
White	235	58	78	99
	(5.3)	(4.0)	(6.0)	(9.0)
Black	114	42	35	37
	(9.2)	(10.2)	(10.6)	(14.2)
Divorced	315	111	130	74
	(5.6)	(5.9)	(7.9)	(5.4)
White	244	84	100	60
	(5.5)	(5.7)	(7.6)	(5.4)
Black	71	27	30	14
	(5.7)	(6.5)	(9.1)	(5.4)
Separated	292	152	76	64
	(5.2)	(8.1)	(4.6)	(4.7)
White	165	82	39	44
	(3.8)	(5.6)	(3.0)	(4.0)
Black	127	70	37	20
	(10.3)	(17.0)	(11.2)	(7.7)

a. Rates are calculated to be the average number of events of the type per year per 1,000 married women starting the time span.

Furthermore, not all of the women were in their first marriages when selected for the sample. Responses to a 1967 question on previous marriages show that the women who would experience one or more marital transitions while participating in the study were much more likely to have already experienced the end of at least one previous marital relationship. The highest proportion in a second or higher order marriage, perhaps not surprisingly, is found among the women who would subsequently divorce (27.5%), followed by women who would separate (24.6%), and those facing death of their spouse (20.1%). In contrast, only 12.2% of the women in the comparison group (those continuously married 1967-1982) were in a second marriage in 1967. Given the age range of the sample when selected (30-44), it is not surprising that 89% of marriages ended prior to the study's inception had been via divorce.

These results and the earlier discussion of the complex marital histories of some respondents suggest the potential for a small group of individuals who we might call "marital movers." These women experience much more mobility into and out of marriage than is usual. Although the number of potential "marital movers" is too small for analysis ($N = 63$ respondents report three or more marriages either before or during the study period), the effects of such a group warrant examination. On a national level marital movers might be responsible for some inflation of the rates of marital dissolution, remarriage, and the higher rate of divorce among remarriages (Cherlin, 1978).

The figures in Table 3.1 can also be examined in terms of racial and time comparisons. Although one fifth of the women in the sample who remained married were black, slightly more (22.5%) of the women who divorced fell into this category. In contrast, however 32.7% of the women who became widowed and a striking 43.5% of those who separated were black! This is substantially higher than their proportion in the sample (29%), and reflects the selective processes by which some women move into one of the formerly married categories. These higher rates of separation and widowhood among black midlife women may reflect cultural differences, income differences, or interactions of these and other effects. The racial disparity between the divorced and the separated confirms earlier studies that women of color were more likely to remain separated for long time periods, rather than moving to divorce under the expensive fault-based legal systems in place in most states during most of the time of the study (Cherlin, 1981).

Examining the data in Table 3.1 by the timing of termination demonstrates some marked variability in the rates of terminations across time. Given what is already known about the typical ages at which people separate, divorce, and enter widowed status, the NLS panel should show decreasing incidence of divorce or separation across time and an increasing rate of widowhood. As expected, the rate of widowhood grew in later intervals of the panel. By 1977, when respondents were 40-54 years of age, higher age-specific death rates were apparently having an influence. The increase in widowhood across time is linear for white women, and raises the already high rate for black women further only in the final five years.

For divorce the expected pattern of decline in rate over time does not clearly appear in the data of Table 3.1. As expected, there were more divorces (in both numbers and rate) in the first five years of the study than in the last five-year span. Instead of decreasing in the middle five years, however, the rate of divorce went higher, with increases for both black and white women. This increase was followed by a drop in the rate of divorce in the third five-year interval for women of both races. One possible explanation of this anomalous pattern is the advent of no-fault divorce provisions being introduced during this time period in many states. Although research finds that no-fault has not had substantial impacts on overall divorce rates (Bahr, 1983), it may have had an impact on the timing of some dissolutions.

In contrast, the number of separations by the third time span is less than half of what it is in the first five years, reflecting lower rates. This decrease is primarily due to a reduced rate of separation among black women. Overall the comparisons in Table 3.1 conform to most expectations regarding both timing and the racial mix of separation, widowhood, and divorce. The upturn in divorce in the middle time period of the study remains something of a mystery but is not so marked as to cause severe concern about the quality of the data. These patterns provide a strong initial sense of the representativeness of the sample for studying marital transitions and any loss of economic protection among midlife women. They further suggest marked variation among groups in racial composition that must be kept in mind for subsequent comparisons.

Age

Effects of age have already been shown indirectly in the figures on the rates of marital termination across time. Age is an important factor in itself, and may shape or be related to the extent of economic dependency or risk factors for poverty, including the presence of young dependent children, experience in the labor force, level of education, and attitudes toward marriage and women's roles.

The midlife women in this sample represent cohorts born between 1923 and 1937, a relatively limited range. Significant differences may appear, even within the age range of 15 years. Differences in age among widowed, separated, and divorced women may translate into different choices and behaviors, regardless of the way in which their marriages ended.

Table 3.2 lists the average ages at termination of marriage for each of the three groups in total and broken down by race. Comparisons among groups show the expected difference for widowed women, with mean ages approximately two to four years higher than for those women who separate or divorce. Women who would experience divorce or separation during the study were approximately the same ages, on the average, when these events were initiated. Differences by race are very small for the divorced, but slightly larger for the separated and widowed, where they reach statistical significance. White women were both separated and widowed at slightly

Table 3.2 Average Ages of Women at Marital Transition by Prospective Marital Group and Race[a]

	Total	White	Black
Prospective Marital Group			
Widowed	46.3 (349)[c]	46.9 (235)	45.0 (114)[b]
Divorced	42.3 (315)	42.2 (244)	42.4 (71)
Separated	42.4 (292)	43.3 (165)	41.2 (127)[b]

a. Age at marital transition is the respondent's age at final interview before her marital transition, and thus is an approximation of her age at the time her marriage ended.
b. Differences by race in this marital category are statistically significant ($p < .01$).
c. Differences between average age of widows and the other two groups are statistically significant ($p < .01$), but the divorced and separated are not significantly different from one another.

older ages than their black counterparts. In examining the figures for the divorced, however, it should be noted that the subgroup who had separated prior to divorce were older at divorce (Mean = 43.8 years) than those who moved directly to divorce (Mean = 41.5 years), with the pattern holding at statistically significant levels for women of both races. Thus women who separate first reach the onset of divorced status approximately 2-2.5 years older than women who move directly into divorced status.

Examination of the range of ages at which the marital transitions occurred shows all three happening at virtually the full range of possible ages within the NLS sample (32-59 years). What differs is the distribution of women across this age range for each group. The differences shown in Table 3.2 are the combined result of the fact that widowhoods happened later during the study and that divorcing and separating women were younger when the study began in 1967.

It is reassuring that the average age differences are in the anticipated direction and are not overly large. These NLS figures compare with an average age for widowhood of 67.6 and of 29.7 years for divorce in 1976 (U.S. Bureau of the Census, 1987d; U.S. Dept. of Health and Human Services, 1980). Given the age restrictions of the sample, the sample differences should be much smaller than those in the overall population, where divorces can and do happen before the 30s and widowhoods predominantly occur after age 60.

Although the NLS sample does not capture the full range of divorce and widowhood experience because of the truncated age range, it presents

Table 3.3 Completed Years of Education as of 1967 by Prospective Marital Group and Race

	Total		*White*		*Black*	
Prospective Marital Group [a]						
Years of School Completed						
Married						
0-8 Years	15.8	(463)	12.2	(290)	31.5	(173)[b]
9-11 Years	21.3	(624)	19.2	(457)	30.7	(169)
12 Years	45.0	(1,319)	49.2	(1,171)	26.9	(148)
13-15 Years	9.2	(268)	10.3	(244)	4.4	(24)
16+ Years	8.6	(252)	9.1	(216)	6.5	(36)
Widowed						
0-8 Years	28.2	(98)	20.0	(47)	45.1	(51)[b]
9-11 Years	23.9	(83)	20.4	(49)	31.0	(35)
12 Years	37.4	(130)	47.2	(111)	16.8	(19)
13-15 Years	6.6	(23)	8.9	(21)	1.8	(2)
16+ Years	4.0	(14)	3.4	(8)	5.3	(6)
Divorced						
0-8 Years	14.6	(46)	11.1	(27)	26.8	(19)[b]
9-11 Years	21.9	(69)	19.3	(47)	31.0	(22)
12 Years	44.4	(140)	48.8	(119)	29.6	(21)
13-15 Years	10.5	(33)	12.3	(30)	4.2	(3)
16+ Years	8.6	(27)	8.6	(21)	8.5	(6)
Separated						
0-8 Years	28.1	(82)	22.4	(37)	35.4	(45)[b]
9-11 Years	25.0	(73)	17.6	(29)	34.6	(44)
12 Years	36.3	(106)	44.2	(73)	26.0	(33)
13-15 Years	6.2	(18)	9.1	(15)	2.4	(3)

a. Differences between the married and divorced are not statistically significant. Nor are differences between the widowed and separated, but the two sets of marital categories differ on education from one another at $p < .001$.
b. Differences by race are statistically significant ($p < .01$).

advantages. By limiting the age range we also limit the variation due to age and cohort differences that have so confounded comparative research in the past. The group differences in age at transition, although minor, will need to be taken into account in future discussions of changes following the termination of marriage.

Education

The next baseline factor to be examined is educational attainment. Education serves both as a reflection of the characteristics of the woman herself and the married couple to which she belongs, and is also a key factor in determination of "human capital." Thus it may be key to outcomes following separation, widowhood, and divorce.

Highly educated women are not simply able to earn higher wages, but also are more likely to have employment experience and greater stability/job security. If, as has been argued, higher earnings serve as an enabling condition for divorce (Houseknecht & Spanier, 1980), we would expect to find higher educational attainment among women who divorced compared to those who were separated or widowed. We should also anticipate that age differences would be reflected in lower educational attainment for widows and among black women. Table 3.3 displays the years of completed education for the various marital groups as of 1967, since relatively little additional education occurred during the study period.

Examining the distribution of educational attainment by marital transition group and race in Table 3.3 reveals many of the anticipated differences. Among all four marital status groups the modal category is a high school education, with the divorced and married having the largest proportions at high school graduate level (44.4% and 45% respectively). The separated and widowed have smaller percentages with high school diplomas. These differences, however, go much deeper. More of the married and divorced groups (17.8% and 19.1% respectively) have at least some college or have gone further in education, compared to approximately 10% of widows and separated women.

Correspondingly, more of the widowed and separated groups have had less than high school educations (52.5% and 53.1% respectively). It should be mentioned, however, that even among the married and the divorced about 36% of the women had completed less than a high school diploma. Educational attainment figures for the separated show them to be very similar to the widowed, although the divorced more closely resemble the married women, and differences between these two sets of marital groups are significant.

A more detailed pattern appears when differences by race are considered. Black women in each of the four prospective marital categories have significantly lower levels of educational attainment in 1967 than their white counterparts. Black widows are the most disadvantaged, with three quarters of their numbers (75.9%) having less than a high school education. In the other three marital status groups, women of color fare only slightly better. Examining the white women shows that very similar proportions (44.2% to 49.2%) had completed high school. Fewer of the widowed and separated groups had education beyond high school, but the differences among the groups of white women are smaller than those for the category totals. Race makes a great deal of difference in levels of educational attainment across marital status groups. For widows, where there are striking differences between white and black women, the effect of racial composition on group totals is most noticeable. The data for both the separated and widowed suggest that their lower overall level of educational attainment is largely due to the very high proportion of less educated women of color in their ranks.

It cannot be concluded that lower levels of education lead to widowhood and separation, while higher levels lead to divorce or continuing marriage. There remain too many other factors that may be implicated in these relationships to draw such a conclusion. The results shown in Table 3.3, however, do not refute the argument that education may be an enabling factor for women in unhappy marriages to move to divorce. The data show that women who separate prior to divorce are no different in educational attainment than those moving directly to divorce. Women who only separate, without divorcing, however, have lower levels of education as a group.

Comparable population information from the Bureau of the Census shows the modal level of educational attainment for these cohorts of women is high school graduation with years of schooling just short of and just beyond that level typical (U.S. Bureau of the Census, 1987d). The NLS sample compares favorably with these population estimates.

Current Employment and Work Attitudes

This section examines both the labor force activity of NLS women and their attitudes toward employment prior to the ending of their marriages. The attitudes questions, although asking about work among women in general, may also reflect the respondent's own willingness to undertake paid employment. Alternatively, labor force attitudes may serve as a proxy for gender-role beliefs. These behavioral and attitudinal baselines are important for later analyses of labor force changes by women who, through circumstances often beyond their control, will be faced with key decisions about employment after their marriages end.

Differences in race, age, and education already discussed were expected to translate into variation in current labor force participation and attitudes regarding work. For example, women facing widowhood may be somewhat

Table 3.4 Activity Survey Week by Prospective Marital Group (Time0)[a]

| | Prospective Marital Group[d] | | | |
	Married	Widowed	Divorced	Separated
Activity in Survey Week				
Employed (Total)	49.1	54.1	66.5	60.4
White	46.8[c]	52.8	63.9	61.3
Black	60.2	56.6	75.8	59.1
Unemployed	2.3	2.5	4.6	5.3
Keeping House	43.8	36.5	25.6	28.3
Other[b]	4.8	6.9	4.3	5.3

a. Data based on the final interview prior to marital transitions.

b. "Other" category includes going to school, unable to work, retired and an "other" response.

c. Difference by race for the married statistically significant at $p < .001$.

d. Marital status differences that reach statistical significance are married/divorced ($p < .0001$), married/separated ($p < .0001$), and widowed/divorced ($p < .01$).

more traditional in their views and less likely to be employed during marriage due to being older or having less education. Other studies would lead us to anticipate that divorcing women would be more work oriented in both attitudes and behavior (Bianchi & Spain, 1986). Because relatively less is known about women experiencing separation, it is difficult to predict specifically their labor force activity or attitudes. The responses and actions of the NLS respondents should be understood in the somewhat more traditional temporal context of the late 1960s and 1970s during which these data were collected.

Table 3.4 describes the primary activity of respondents during the survey week of the Time0 interview. For the married, the figures represent a randomized Time0, to reduce any temporal effects on these activities from selecting a single year for comparison. At the times of these interviews, when all respondents were married, varying percentages across marital groups were employed, ranging from less than half (49.1%) of those who would remain married to two thirds (66.5%) among the divorced with the separated and widowed holding intermediate levels of employment (60.4% and 54.1%, respectively). Low levels of all groups were unemployed or involved in activities other than the major choices of working or keeping house.

Keeping house mirrors the employment statistics, with the most women from the married group (43.8%) involved, and the lowest percentage (25.6%) among the divorced. Unlike education, here the married and divorced are most dissimilar, while the married and widowed groups are more alike. Differences among marital groups are statistically significant, with the exception of the comparison of the widowed/separated and the widowed/divorced.

Examining employment patterns by race once again changes the picture. All four groups of black women have, as expected, higher levels of participation in the labor force than their white counterparts. The degree to which race makes a difference varies across groups, from a 2.0% difference among the separated to a 13.4% difference among the married, the only such difference that is statistically significant.

We might speculate that a few of the women had sought employment in order to prepare themselves due to advance warning or suspicion of the impending end of marriage. Comparing the data on the interview previous to the Time0 measurement shows that all groups had increased their labor force involvement before this time, following the national trend toward increasing involvement of midlife women in work. The smallest increase from the prior interview was for the married (4.9%), followed by the separated (5.9%) and the widowed (6.3%). Among the divorced, however, there was a striking 11% increase in labor force activity from the prior (Time–1) to the final interview prior to termination of marriage. It seems likely that midlife women anticipating divorce were making some adaptations to their expected change of marital status, over and above the general movement toward the labor force among women. This argument is further bolstered by examination of two subgroups among the divorced: those who had been separated prior to divorce and those who moved directly into divorce from marriage. Divorcing women who had separated had only a very small increase in labor force involvement prior to Time0 (.7%), although women who moved more directly to divorce had a 15.9% increase from the interview prior to Time0 (to 65.6%). These results suggest that women who separated had made their preparatory labor force adjustments earlier, while women just preparing to divorce began moving into the labor force in earnest during their final year or two of marriage.

Data on sheer labor force participation tell only part of the story, because hours of work can also be augmented by those moving toward greater economic independence. The data on the hours worked in the survey week (Time0) show some variation across marital categories, from 86% of the divorced down to 66% of the married working full-time (defined here as 35 or more hours per week). The percentages for the widowed and separated were 70.6% and 76.6%, respectively. There were no significant differences by race nor had the level of full-time work changed from the prior interview. Thus anticipatory changes that occurred appear largely to be movement into the labor force, rather than increase in the number of hours worked.

Data presented in Table 3.4 provide some interesting basic information but little insight into the orientations of the women in this sample toward the

Table 3.5 Attitudes Toward Current Job and Women Working by Prospective
Marital Group and Race

		Prospective Marital Group		
	Married	*Widowed*	*Divorced*	*Separated*
Workers Liking Current Job "Very Much" (%)				
Total	62.0	58.5	61.6	61.7
White	62.6	57.1	61.5	64.3
Black	59.9	61.4	62.1	58.0
Attitude Toward Women Working If:[a]				
Necessary to Make Ends Meet				
Total	4.4	4.3	4.6	4.5
White	4.4	4.3	4.6	4.5
Black	4.3	4.4	4.5	4.5
She Desires/Husband Agrees				
Total	3.9[b]	4.0	4.2	4.2
White	3.9	3.8	4.2	4.1
Black	4.1	4.2	4.3	4.2
She Desires/Husband Disagrees				
Total	2.1[b]	2.2	2.4	2.4
White	2.0	2.1	2.4	2.4
Black	2.3	2.3	2.4	2.5

a. Average score on item for the women in the category when 1 = Definitely not all right and 5 = Definitely
all right.
b. Difference by race within this marital category significant at $p < .01$.

labor force. Are there differences in these orientations according to their
marital futures? The NLS has limited data to address the question of attitude
and orientation. Table 3.5 presents figures for attitudinal variables pertaining
to orientations to work. The first asked midlife women who were currently
employed to rate how they felt about their current jobs. The distribution of
responses was very skewed toward the positive side. This positive reaction
to current jobs does not vary by prospective marital status in 1967, with
proportions who "like(d) it very much" ranging from 61% among the
separated and divorced to 58% among the widowed. There were no significant differences by race or by prospective marital group, with very similar
percentages reporting favorable reactions to their current jobs. Although we
might have anticipated lower job satisfaction among black women, reflecting
lower pay and less advantaged working conditions more common among
women of color, their evaluations of their current jobs were quite similar to
those reported by white women.

The second set of items in Table 3.5 is the scores on three attitude items on women's employment in general. This set of questions was included in 1967, 1972, and 1977, and thus reflects the respondents' attitudes within the five years prior to their transitions out of marriage. The questions asked all NLS respondents what they thought (definitely all right = 5 to definitely not all right = 1) about women working: (1) if it was necessary to make ends meet; (2) if the woman desired and her husband agreed; and (3) if she desired and her husband disagreed. As might be anticipated, the level of agreement diminished significantly from the first to the third question. Women in all marital categories thought it was probably or definitely all right for a woman to work if it was necessary to make ends meet. Beyond the area of necessity, however, approval diminished. Typical scores on the second item were in the neighborhood of 4 ("probably all right"), and for the third item, "if her husband disagrees," scores were significantly lower, so that average group scores hover around 2 ("probably not all right"). Examination of differences across prospective marital categories and race show remarkably little variation. Although some of the comparisons by race and marital group are statistically significant, with black women and the divorced and separated groups slightly more positive toward women working than their married or widowed peers, the magnitude of these attitude differences is small.

These findings do not address whether the NLS women believe that working was appropriate for themselves in their current family and economic circumstances. Unfortunately, no such questions were included in the instrument. Nor do questions specifically address the attitudes toward women working once their marriages have ended. Presumably the argument of financial necessity, found in the first of the three attitude items, would apply to many such circumstances and suggest positive attitudes generally to women working following divorce, separation, or widowhood.

An interesting addendum to these attitude items are two questions asked in 1967 about husbands' attitudes toward wives working. The first asked working women their husbands' attitudes about their current job. The average response across all categories varied between "liking it somewhat" and "undecided." There was no variation by race or by marital category, suggesting an unusually high level of consensus across groups on how their husbands' viewed their jobs. When women who were not currently employed were asked their husbands' attitudes toward them starting to work, the average answer, again with only minimal variation by marital category, averaged near the "dislike it somewhat" response category. There were, however, differences by race for this question. Husbands of nonemployed white women were reported by their wives to be more negative toward their starting to work than were husbands of black women, with average responses in the latter category hovering around the slightly more positive "undecided" response. In general, then, husbands appear to be less positive toward wives' work (in the view of the respondents) than they themselves are. These more negative attitudes of husbands may play a role in the labor force decisions of married women. After marriage ends, however, any disincentive presented by the husband's negative attitudes departs and the pressures to provide independent income grow.

Family and Children

Women who fall into the various marital transition categories may also differ from one another in important ways with regard to their family configurations. Both family size and the ages of children may make a substantial difference in the financial needs and the employment patterns of women once they are no longer married. NLS women experiencing widowhood may, because of somewhat higher ages themselves, have slightly older children and be closer to completion of their child-rearing years. Divorcing and separated women may have larger families or younger children. These differences in household structure derive not only from age differences at the transition event, but also potentially from variation in composition of the groups by race, educational level, or other differences.

This section examines dependent children in the household, in terms of their numbers and ages. There are some variations by marital category and also some by race, but again all differences are relatively muted compared to those that might be found in the general population of widowed, separated, and divorced women (see Table 3.6). Future widows are more likely to report no dependent children at their last pre-widowhood interview. The divorced and separated categories report somewhat larger pretransition families (more women with three or more children) than the widows, but are not significantly different from the distribution for married women. In terms of differences by race, three of the four groups show statistically significant differences in numbers of children (the exception is the divorced group). Women of color are typically more concentrated in the upper end of the distribution, with more of them having large (four or more children) families. The difference is most noticeable for the separated, where about 40% of black women have four or more children compared to 19% of white women who separate. Again these numbers need to be placed in the context of the late 1960s and through the early 1980s when data were collected. Family sizes

Table 3.6 Number of Dependents by Prospective Marital Group and Race

	0	1	2	3	4+
			Number of Dependents[c]		
Prospective Marital Group[b]					
Married[a]	15.4	18.0	25.7	19.0	29.2
White	14.7	18.5	26.4	19.2	21.2
Black	19.1	15.1	21.5	17.9	26.3
Widowed[a]	25.3	26.3	13.9	13.4	21.1
White	29.5	33.6	13.9	12.3	10.7
Black	18.1	13.9	13.9	15.3	38.9
Divorced	12.3	15.1	33.5	15.1	24.0
White	13.7	14.4	33.8	15.8	22.3
Black	7.5	17.5	32.5	12.5	30.0
Separated[a]	14.3	16.5	22.0	18.7	28.6
White	15.8	17.8	28.7	18.8	18.8
Black	12.3	14.8	13.6	18.5	40.7

a. Differences by race are statistically significant at $p < .02$.
b. Differences are statistically significant when comparing the married to the widowed ($p < .001$), the widowed with the divorced ($p < .001$), the widowed and the separated ($p < .01$), and marginally significant for the divorced and separated ($p < .05$).
c. The questions used to assess this factor varied over time. The interest was in the number of dependents in the household, but these questions were not asked in 1974 and 1976. For years up to 1974 dependents outside the household were subtracted from total dependents, although from 1977-1981 number of dependents in the household was asked directly.

that seem large by today's standard were much more normative during this time period.

These findings mean that the great majority of women who experience marital transitions do so with at least one dependent child in the household. Because effects of having dependent children are mediated by their ages, the next question is whether there were differences in the age of the youngest child for midlife women prior to termination of marriage.

The expectation that the children of women in the widowed group would be older, given the higher ages in this category, is borne out by Table 3.7. Nearly half (46.2%) of widows had a youngest child who was a teen, compared to 30%-35% of the other three marital groups. In contrast, the preschool category (under age 6) ranges from 21.2% for widows to a high of 30.1% among the separated. Differences by marital category are only selectively significant (i.e., comparing the married

Table 3.7 Age of Youngest Child Among Those with Children by Prospective Marital Group and Race

| | Age of Youngest Child[a] | | |
	6 or Younger	7-12 Years	13 or Older
Married (N = 1,301)	25.6	43.9	30.5
White	25.4	44.8	29.8
Black	26.9	37.2	35.9
Widowed (N = 132)	21.2	32.6	46.2
White	16.7	32.1	46.2
Black	27.8	33.3	38.9
Divorced (N = 148)	22.3	46.6	31.1
White	22.6	47.0	30.4
Black	21.2	45.5	33.3
Separated (N = 143)	30.1	35.0	35.0
White	23.3	41.1	35.6
Black	37.1	28.6	34.3

a. The NLS asked this question only up through 1972. Given the manner in which it was coded (e.g., children 0-2, 3-5, and 14-17) it is difficult to impute ages for a youngest child beyond that year. And because some women might have had additional children after 1972, women whose pretransition time falls after 1972 are not included in this table, significantly reducing the sample sizes (indicated). It is not required in the question that this youngest child be in the household of the respondent.

to the widowed and the widowed to the divorced), and there are no significant differences by race.

These comparisons show us that not only do most women approach the end of their marriages with children in the household, but also that from one fifth to nearly one third of those with children have a child of preschool age just prior to marital termination. This means that their transitions will be complicated by the need for and costs of child care if they plan to work, or decisions to remain at home with their associated income, human capital, and social costs.

SUMMARY AND IMPLICATIONS

The comparisons in this chapter point out one very important conclusion that must be taken forward to the subsequent analyses. The conclusion is that women who will experience the various marital transitions differed in important ways from one another and from women who would remain married well prior to the ending of their marriages. Many of the differences are small but some are quite noteworthy. There are also many systematic differences by race that argue for caution in comparisons across marital status groups given their varying racial compositions. These NLS women are diverse not only in the forms of marital termination they will experience, but also in their life experience and traits during marriage. Many of the differences in characteristics may be associated causally or coincidentally with their probability of experiencing a transition out of marriage or the type of transition they will face (i.e., being separated vs. being widowed). Their backgrounds during marriage may significantly shape the economic and social consequences they experience after marriage, and the type of adaptations they make. In comparing the three transitional groups, widows are somewhat older, less educated, as likely to be employed and like their jobs, and slightly less likely to have children or young children. The divorced are more educated, most likely to be employed in marriage, and quite likely to have children, including young children. The separated appear to be the least advantaged, having the lowest educational attainment, significantly more black women in their ranks, and are more likely to have a large family or a child under six years of age.

For us, however, it is imperative to keep in mind that there are differences aside from marital status change that make these groups somewhat distinctive. In examining what happens to them following the ending of their marriages, partitioning out the variation that predates the end of marriage becomes essential. For example, care must be taken not to attribute high rates of labor force involvement among the divorced as the effect purely of marital dissolution, because they clearly worked more during marriage and had higher levels of education, enabling employment. In other words, the differences found in most of the traits that have been examined here are important controls in the analyses that follow. Although major comparisons are drawn systematically by the type of marital transition and race, other factors such as education, family size, age, or attitudes may be used as explanatory or control factors in many of the specific comparisons of outcomes. In this way it is possible to avoid spuriously attributing changes that are really preexisting differences or correlated factors to the end of marriage. These findings sound an important cautionary note, because we cannot simply compare the groups to each other and to the married group to determine the effects of marital termination. That would fold into the comparison the differences that existed for them beforehand and potentially exaggerate the apparent effects of the ending of marriage.

This is a flaw in many cross-sectional analyses, which seem to assume that before their marriages ended all women were equal. Here we see that is not the case. Failing to examine differences by social class, race, and other factors that differentiate both between and within these groups leads to incorrect conclusions and oversimplification. In the next chapter a careful examination of changes over time begins, with initial explorations of changes in income, assets, and economic well-being following separation, widowhood, and divorce.

NOTES

1. There is a weighting scheme provided by the NLS to correct for this overrepresentation of black women. The sample, when weighted, is representative of the noninstitutionalized female population of the country at the time the sample was drawn (Center for Human Resource Research, 1983). The consequences, however, of using a sample weighting system are unknown when dealing with relatively small subgroups out of the total sample, such as the groups experiencing separation, widowhood, or divorce in this analysis. Reducing the impact of the black women respondents through weighting would also not permit adequate estimates of the circumstances of black women as they move through transitions out of marriage. Therefore, it was decided to forgo the use of the weighting system and, instead, to use comparisons by race or to employ proper caution in interpreting the results on unweighted groups containing both black and white women.

2. In the questionnaires, the midlife women were asked detailed questions regarding income, assets, and earnings that serve as the primary bases for examination of economic change following marital termination. Not all income questions were identical in all surveys. Typically, respondents were asked to provide income amounts for the prior calendar year separately for self and other members of the household, although some separated self, spouse, and others in the household. For each of these categories income was detailed separately in most years for wages, unemployment compensation, Social Security retirement, disability, worker's compensation, Social Security disability or other disability income, or pension. In addition, respondents were asked if they or other members of their households received income from farm operation, business or partnership, rentals to roomers or boarders, interest or dividends on investments, food stamps, Aid to Families with Dependent Children, Supplemental Security Income, alimony, child support, income from other family members, royalties or annuities, or any other source. In some years several of these categories were collapsed together into a single question or grouped into a category for "other sources of income," but the intent of the designers was to elicit comparable information across various interviews regarding total amounts and major source categories. Any variation that occurred in income reporting based on these varying response formats was randomized relative to when the transitions of separation, widowhood, or divorce occurred, likely creating no systematic biases relative to these events.

Total household or family income, used in subsequent comparisons and as the basis for assessing poverty levels, was computed by adding the dollar amounts for each of the available income categories for all household members in the prior calendar years. All figures were corrected for inflation to 1981 equivalence using adjustments based on the Consumer Price

Index. Respondents were presumed to be reporting honestly and as correctly as possible regarding income and its specific sources. Despite efforts to minimize error by focusing on specific information in the questions, there is undoubtedly some error in these reports. It is assumed to be nonsystematic and limited in its effects.

Another major category, assets, was evaluated in several interviews by asking respondents about money in several types of savings or investments (saving and checking accounts, savings and loan companies, or credit unions), owned value of U.S. savings bonds, stocks, bonds, or shares in mutual funds, money owed to the respondent by others, equity in the current home or other real estate or a farm that is owned. These data are summed to create a total assets amount, which for most respondents is fairly small and composed primarily of home equity and bank accounts. (See also notes in Chapter 4.)

3. In fact, a few of the separated women ($N = 7$) had husbands who subsequently died during the separation. This pattern is atypical but demonstrates the diversity of outcomes possible in a large and random sample of midlife women.

4

Changing Economic Fortunes of Women After Marriage

Having established diversity in the circumstances and traits of women approaching the end of marriage, we now turn to the financial consequences of divorce, widowhood, and separation. In this chapter the focus is on changes, both short and longer term, in economic status for midlife women departing marriage, evaluated in terms of total family income, poverty rates, and sources of income. Previous research leads to a strong expectation of shifts on all of these dimensions for women upon the end of marriage.

In this chapter several related questions are addressed. First, do midlife women face significant declines in their economic well-being after marriage ends? Second, how common and persistent a problem is poverty in the years after divorce, widowhood, or separation? Third, how do the changing sources of income, with their linkages to social policies, shape economic well-being among formerly married women? Fourth, what other characteristics of midlife women are important in shaping these outcomes after marriage ends? That is, are characteristics such as race, education, employment status, family size, and so on important in understanding which women thrive or suffer financially after marriage ends? Built into all of the sections are contrasts between widowed, separated, and divorced women.

FAMILY INCOME AND ASSETS

Short-Term Changes in Income Levels

Total family income is the sum of income from all sources to respondent, spouse, and other family members living in the household in the completed calendar year preceding the interview.[1] With departure from marriage a woman and any dependent children she may have in her custody lose the bulk of the income that had been provided by the husband. The data on median family income before marital transitions (Time0 in Table 4.1) show rather substantial differences in average income levels among the groups just prior to the end of their marriages. The married comparison group were already the best off, followed by the divorcing group. Widowed and separated women, however, had lower median income at the final interview during marriage. All four groups included a wide range of incomes with some rather well-to-do and some financially strapped households among their numbers. The medians, however, suggest that in the aggregate the separating and soon-to-be widowed start off with something of an income disadvantage just in advance of marital termination.

Widowed, divorced, and separated groups all demonstrated substantial declines in median income at the first interview after their marriages ended. In fact, these changes diminished the differences among the group medians from over $8,000 to about $5,200. The divorced women continued to have the highest income levels in the short term, experiencing on average a 29% decline from their prior income. Two distinct patterns emerge when those who separated prior to divorce are compared to the other new divorcees. Although the individuals who moved directly from marriage to divorce had a large average decline in family income (39.3%), women who had been separated actually saw their incomes improve slightly, on average, after divorce (3.3% improvement). Clearly, placing these two groups of newly divorced women together mutes the income decline that appears for the category overall. Recall, however, that because these are average changes, many of the women who had separated before divorcing may still experience further income decline as well as modest improvement.

Median income for the widowed group declined by 33%, although the decline for the separated was only 23%. Thus the group with the highest pretransition incomes (the divorced) lost the most, while the more limited incomes of the separated encountered the smallest relative reduction, perhaps bolstered by a floor of support from earnings and AFDC. The

Table 4.1 Median Total Family Income Before and After Marital Termination and
Median Percent of Income Decline by Marital Group

	Interview Time Period		Median % Income Decline [a]
	Time0	Time1	
Widowed ($N = 285$)	$18,460	$10,729	35
Divorced ($N = 275$)	$23,890	$15,960	29[b]
Separated ($N =253$)	$15,774	$11,242	23
Married ($N = 2198$)	$27,425	$27,553	-2[c]

a. These figures were calculated by comparing the income of each respondent at the first measurement after transition to her last measurement before transition and averaging the results, rather than being based on the aggregate figures.
b. NLS women who had been separated prior to divorce saw a slight improvement in their median percentage income decline after divorce (–3.3%). Median income for this group ($N = 96$) moved from $13,371 to $13,093, lower postdivorce incomes than those among women who moved more directly into divorce. That group, moving from $28,547 to $15,960, experienced a 39.3% median decline in income over this time span.
c. Represents a small increase over the time period, after correction for inflation.

married group, with a randomly selected hypothetical "before" and "after,"
on the other hand, maintains its income level showing a small increase
across the comparable span of time, as we would expect with career
advancement, more wives becoming employed, and so on.

Although the average trend is to lowered income, each group has
respondents whose incomes improve shortly after marriage ends. A substantial number of the divorced (32%) showed short-term improvement,
but it is not simply the women who had first separated and then divorced
who show such improvement. In the other marital groups improvement
was also apparent for a substantial minority of women (29% among the
widowed and 35% among the separated). Improving income sounds
counterintuitive until one considers the wide range of conditions under
which these midlife marriages ended. These include households that
may have suffered financial distress or behavioral problems such as
drug use or gambling that contributed to dissolution. Examination of
data on widows showed that some whose incomes improved had
reported health problems for their husbands that impaired his capacity
to work (or even hers if she was providing health care) before his death.
Alternatively, improvement may simply reflect the vagaries of economic life that influence many households over time, such as losing a
job, a failed business or farm crop, or a child's serious health problems
that disrupts employment. Some of the improvements also undoubtedly reflect the addition of new income sources available to these

formerly married women. These will be discussed in more detail in a later section of this chapter.

Total Family Income Changes
Over the Long Term

The information presented thus far suggests striking short-term decreases in income for most women whose marriages end. But do these changes persist over time or are they only temporary? Some prior discussions have suggested that there is a "dip and recovery" pattern in income after separation, widowhood, or divorce for women. If this "dip and recovery" occurs there should be an improvement in subsequent interviews, moderating the short-term negative impact.

Figure 4.1 displays changes in total family income by marital group from the baseline year (Time0) to each of the subsequent five interviews. These results graphically show the postmarital income dip with the dramatic downturns for all three transitional groups. Our question now, however, is whether there is a recovery and, if so, its magnitude and timing among midlife women who are divorced, widowed, or separated.

Median income levels across the remaining interviews in Figure 4.1 do not reveal any substantial recovery over time. These income amounts, with minor variations, remain unchanged even at the fifth posttransition measurement point, 7-8 years after marriages ended. With the effects of inflation removed, income levels for the three groups are virtually unchanged many years after the marriages end. The divorced group continues to have the highest and the separated the lowest levels of income. This consistency can also be shown on the individual level by the percentage each woman's income has declined (compared to Time0) by the third post transition interview (five years) and by the fifth interview (7-8 years). For widows the five-year decline is approximately 40% and at the final interview (Time5) is 35%. For the divorced the comparable percentages are slightly lower (33% and 32%, respectively) although the low initial income drop for the separated is mirrored in long-term declines of 25% and 30%. Although there are differences in Time0 income between the divorced women who had already separated and those who moved directly into divorce, both groups, after having experienced their initial declines, reported consistent income amounts in the remaining interviews. Apparently the income change for the women who separated and then divorced really took place at separation, so that the very limited

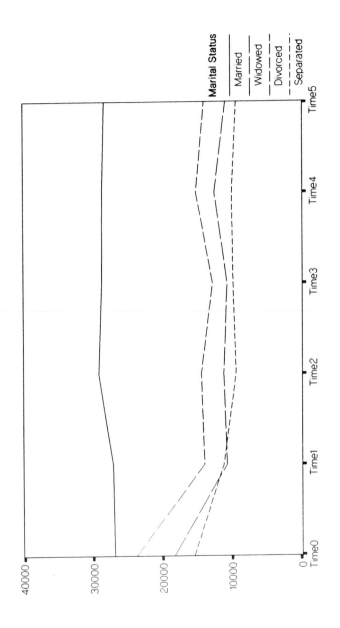

Figure 4.1. Median Total Family Over Time by Martial Status

"recovery" at divorce for some of these women was not the precursor of continuing improvement over time.

As a basis for comparison, however, it is essential to examine the changes in the married group. This group shows remarkable stability in median income over time. The married were managing to keep up with inflation during this period, and even gain slightly. Overall, Figure 4.1 suggests that for those women who remain separated, widowed, or divorced for relatively long periods of time, the income outlook is not a rosy one.

There is, however, another possible contributor to the pattern of unchanging postmarital incomes seen in Figure 4.1. The number of respondents markedly declines across interviews, as the sample runs up against the 1982 end point, as women move out of the groups through attrition, or move into another marital category. Absence of a recovery could potentially be an artifact of another selective process. For example, if higher income women are more likely to remarry or drop out, change over time reflects the modified composition of the group under study. If there is such a selective process, this flattened long-term income trend could artificially mask a recovery happening to the poorer individuals who remain. A separate analysis was performed including only those individuals who continued in their changed marital status for the full five interviews after divorce or widowhood (only 4 interviews for the separated because of higher loss rates). Overall results were very similar to those seen in Figure 4.1. The amount of income decline for all three groups was slightly less dramatic from before to just after the marital transition. After marriages ended, however, income remained essentially unchanged over time. Significantly, there was neither recovery nor additional decline in total family income levels after several years. Thus the findings in Figure 4.1 are not a result of changing composition that selectively removed individuals from the samples over time. This does suggest, however, that women who remain in formerly married statuses for longer periods of time are somewhat different in their characteristics from their peers who remarry or leave the sample group in some other way.[2] It is impossible to say whether those who are lost from the ranks of the formerly married would have contributed stable, improving, or declining incomes had they remained among the unmarried women interviewed over time. What is clear, however, is that for the duration of widowed, divorced, or separated status, the average women in midlife can for the most part expect to see no major improvement in total family income beyond inflation.

Changes in Assets Over Time

Assets, in terms of home equity or bank accounts and invest-ments, can make a major difference in the standard of living for women who have lost the economic protection of marriage. Even those with drastically reduced incomes may, if they have moderate asset resources, be able to cushion the financial blow when their marriages end and largely maintain their lifestyles.

Information on family assets, unlike income, was not collected consis-tently in the NLS panel. In fact, it was included in only five of the interviews (1967, 1971, 1972, 1977, and 1982). Assets were made up of the net value of home, savings, and investments, so that if much is owed it is quite possible to have negative asset values.

The few interviews in which questions on assets were included makes it more difficult to demonstrate confidently a pattern of change over time as midlife women exit from marriage. Responses were further attenuated by the varying times during the study when marital terminations occurred. The comparison of asset levels, covering only three measurements after marriages ended, is in Figure 4.2.

The figures for assets partially confirm patterns for income, in that there are some rather striking differences between groups in the amount of assets accumulated even before marriages end. Individuals who would remain married had the highest median asset amount ($36,674), compared to $14,000-$17,000 for the widowed and divorced groups. Finally, in accord with the other results, the separated respondents had very low assets (median of $4,002) in the final interview prior to the suspension of their marriages.

Assets are thus less available to women who most need them, and most available to the maritally secure. It is not surprising that the separated are so low on assets in comparison to the other groups, because their low incomes and high rates of poverty during marriage precluded the accumulation of resources. Although the divorced have relatively higher incomes than do widows, the widowed (by being older) have had a few more years in which to build assets during marriage. The data also show that the mean value of assets is much higher than the median for all groups, suggesting that in each marital category the distributions of assets are very skewed.

In terms of changes over time, the married group reported modest asset growth, even with dollar amounts corrected for inflation. The widowed, somewhat surprisingly, also demonstrated a growth in assets, albeit not in a linear fashion. This growth may have resulted from insurance settlements or

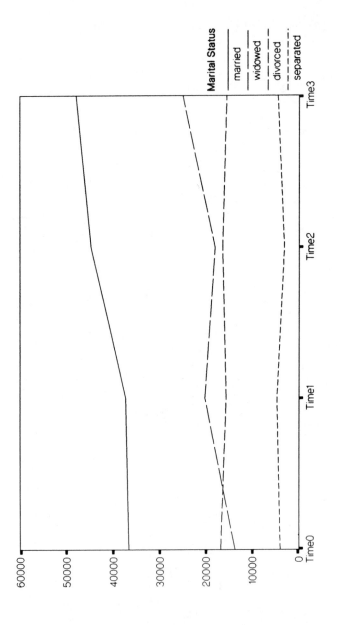

Figure 4.2. Median Assets by Marital Status Over Time

other programs that provide a lump sum benefit, permitting the widow to pay off a mortgage or create investments. The divorcing and separated respondents, however, did not fare as well. Both groups demonstrated essentially no change in median dollars of assets over time. The average separated or divorced woman seemed to be able to hold onto savings and home equity, a situation that may be better than many women see today when assets are often divided 50-50 (Weitzman, 1985). They are not able to save and augment their assets over time. These results should be interpreted very cautiously, given the large amount of missing data.

CHANGES IN POVERTY
FOLLOWING THE END OF MARRIAGE

Another way to examine negative economic consequences of marital termination is through falls into (or near) poverty. Because families of differing sizes and compositions require varying amounts of income in order to meet their basic needs, the poverty level (Orshansky, 1968) provides a standardized means of correcting for such variations. It defines specific dollar amounts required to support minimally families with varying makeup, so that they can be compared. Because marital termination also brings about a reduction (typically by one) of the persons relying on a specified income—a reduction in total family income—say by 35%, does not imply an equivalent reduction in the standard of living. Using the poverty thresholds corrects for this change in composition and also corrects for inflation, through its annual adjustments based on the Consumer Price Index.

Figure 4.3 outlines changing rates of poverty among the four marital status groups across time, from the Time0 interview to the fifth interview after marriages ended,(7-8 years after separation, widowhood, or divorce). Among the married the rate of poverty is lowest and varied only slightly from 9.2% to 11.3% over time. The percentages poor among the separated, widowed, and divorced groups are higher than among the married, both before and after their marital transitions.

The effects from loss of the economic protection of marriage on poverty are notable. The widowed show an increase in poverty from 24% to 34% in Time1, followed by some moderate fluctuations in the levels of poverty in the 26%-36% range. Divorced women do somewhat better, with poverty rates that rise from about 15% to about 18% in Time1, and then vary between 14% and 21%, declining to their original levels by Time5. As with income, there are early differences between the women who separated prior to divorce and those who did not. In Time0 those who had already separated had a

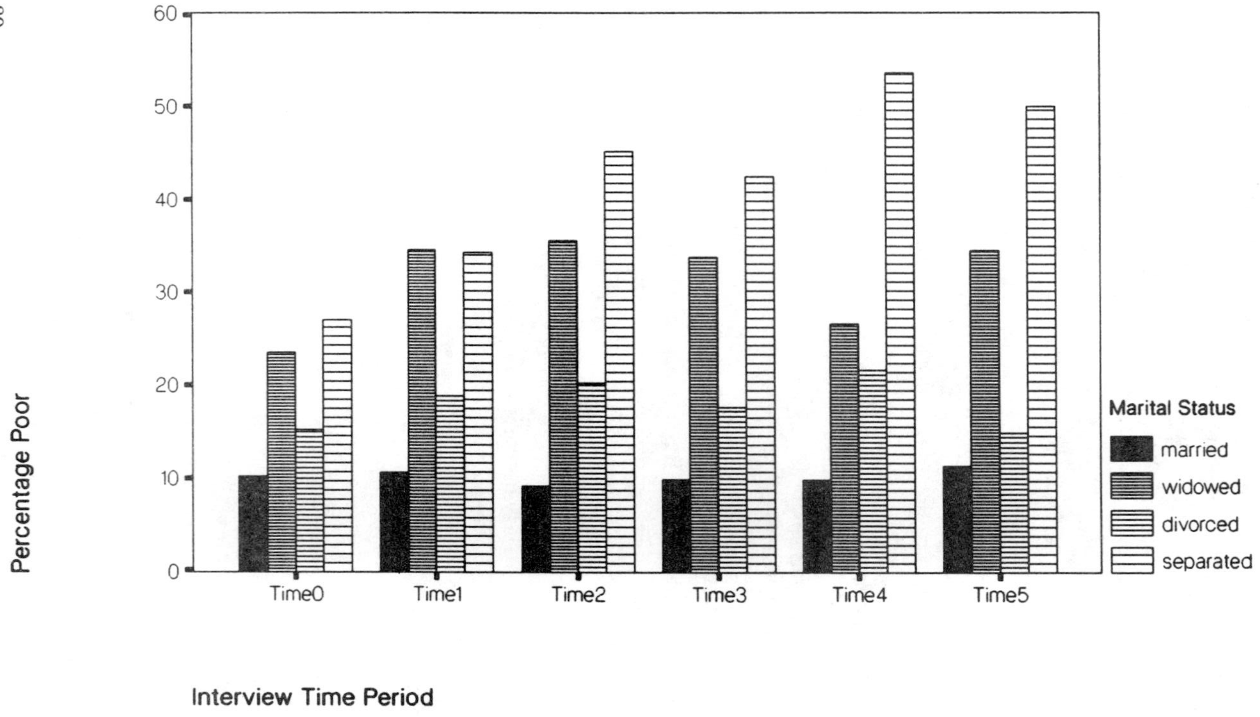

Figure 4.3. Percentage Below the Poverty Level by Marital Status Group and Time Period

poverty rate of 25.7%, compared to only 6.7% among their peers who moved from marriage directly to divorce. This significant difference virtually disappears, however, in all subsequent interviews, in which the risks of poverty are quite similar for these two subgroups of divorced women. The most striking result in these comparisons is the rate of poverty found among women who became separated. This group of midlife women, who have the highest rate of poverty prior to marital transition (27%), move to a peak of poverty of 54% in Time4. These poverty statistics clearly demonstrate that the separated group faces the greatest risk of poverty.

Using poverty rates, however, only examines the lowest end of the income distribution. The poverty level dollar amounts can also be used to create a ratio of income to needs. If total family income is divided by the amount set for the poverty level, relative economic well-being can be compared across families of differing size or composition. Table 4.2 outlines the results of such a comparison, examining the income distribution relative to needs. Here four categories of income relative to needs were created: the *Poor* are those receiving incomes less than the poverty threshold (i.e., the same people included in Figure 4.3); *Marginal* households are those receiving between 100% and 150% of poverty income, indicating financial hardship; *Adequate* households are those in which the family members subsist on income between 150% and 300% of the poverty level; and *Substantial* income households are those that have three times the poverty level income (300%) or more.

Using these categories, it is clear that not only were the married women largely escaping poverty, but that on the whole their income adequacy was good and improving over time. There was, for example, a noticeable growth in the proportion of married women in the *Substantial* income category (48% to 56%). Thus we can conclude that not only are the absolute levels of income of the married households consistently larger across time periods (as was seen in Figure 4.1), but also that these income amounts were more adequate to meet household needs than in other marital status groups. In contrast, the widowed, divorced, and separated groups have reductions in the proportions receiving *Substantial* incomes at marital termination, with slight improvement over time only among the divorced. The widowed have a fairly stable proportion (about one in five) at the *Substantial* level over time, and, as expected, the separated continue to lose ground.

The *Marginal* income category, just above the poverty threshold, is also key to understanding postmarital economic problems. Despite growing numbers of women who have moved into poverty, the ranks of those just above the poverty range do not shrink. Instead they are maintained or enlarged,

Table 4.2 Proportions of Respondents Relative to the Poverty Threshold by
Marital Status Category and Time Period

	Interview Time Period					
	0	1	2	3	4	5
Married						
Poor[a]	10.2	10.6	9.2	9.9	9.8	11.3
Marginal	8.7	7.9	7.8	7.5	6.1	6.1
Adequate	33.1	31.4	29.6	29.0	29.0	26.3
Substantial	48.1	50.1	53.4	53.5	55.0	56.3
Widowed						
Poor	23.5	34.6	36.0	34.5	26.8	34.5
Marginal	12.6	12.6	14.4	14.2	13.7	14.7
Adequate	27.0	29.2	28.4	28.4	35.3	31.9
Substantial	36.9	23.6	21.2	22.8	24.2	19.0
Divorced						
Poor	15.2	18.8	20.2	17.6	21.6	14.9
Marginal	11.1	15.0	15.3	21.4	14.4	17.6
Adequate	32.6	37.6	37.4	30.5	32.0	35.1
Substantial	41.1	28.6	27.1	30.5	32.0	32.4
Separated[b]						
Poor	27.0	34.3	45.2	42.5	53.6	50.0
Marginal	16.3	17.2	15.1	21.9	26.8	23.5
Adequate	30.6	30.5	23.8	24.7	12.5	23.5
Substantial	26.2	18.0	15.9	11.0	7.1	2.9

a. Poor: < 100% of poverty threshold; Marginal: 100-150% of poverty threshold; Adequate: 150-300% of poverty threshold; Substantial: 300% or more of poverty threshold.
b. Numbers for the separated shrink very rapidly over time, so that the figures for the fourth and fifth years are based on only 56 and 34 cases, respectively. Extreme caution must be employed in drawing conclusions.

undoubtedly by women relocating from the *Adequate* or *Substantial* categories. This process is, again, most apparent among the separated, where the percentage with *Marginal* income is highest before separation and the levels increase somewhat over time. Inability to afford a divorce may result in continuing separation, although difficulty in using the court system to gain child support during an informal separation may also contribute to poverty or near-poverty income levels in this group.

Analyses of women with continuous participation after their marriages ended, used to reveal any effects of selective attrition or compositional change on poverty rates, showed some differences from Table 4.2. Among the newly widowed the increase in poverty was more muted, from 30% to 33%. For the separating group, however, there was significantly more poverty both before and after separation, confirming that women who remain separated are among the most economically disadvantaged before as well as after separation. The divorcing women had essentially the same pattern of poverty rates. Thus we might conclude that rates of poverty are somewhat higher than they might have been had other separated or widowed women remained over longer periods of time, instead of remarrying, divorcing or dropping out.

In sum, the risks of poverty are substantially higher for midlife women whose marriages end, regardless of the manner in which they end. Divorcing women face the lowest risks of becoming poor, and the separated the highest. Poverty is not something that only occurs soon after marriage ends and is then "escaped" as the woman/family adapt to their changed circumstances. Even up to seven or eight years after marriages end, an inflated rate of poverty persists for the widowed and separated over that experienced by their married counterparts.

Changes in the Poverty Population

The next question in conjunction with poverty is whether the poor at each postmarital interview are composed of largely the same set of individuals (i.e., is there persistent poverty?). If the NLS data show a smaller group of persistently poor individuals although others of their peers avoid poverty altogether, then the causes may rest in traits of the women and their backgrounds, rather than the changes in income following from the end of marriage. Such personal traits (e.g., education, work experience, race, etc.) should at least partially determine risks of poverty, not simply marital termination.

Figure 4.4 outlines respondents who were poor for one or more surveys by marital category. As expected, the married had the highest proportion escaping poverty altogether (79.9%), followed by the divorced (65.7%). Only approximately half of the separated (51.4%) and the widowed (47.3%) escape at least a brief fall into poverty during their time in the NLS panel. Among those who did become poor, the large number of individuals who were poor in only one time interval suggests that persistent poverty is not the norm.

The separated group, which has appeared to be the most disadvantaged thus far, seems to have an unexpectedly high proportion of individuals who never become poor. This seems at first glance to be inconsistent with the poverty statistics presented earlier in Figure 4.3. Because the separated quickly lose women from their ranks through divorce, reconciliation with their husbands, or dropping out of the study, they do not have the

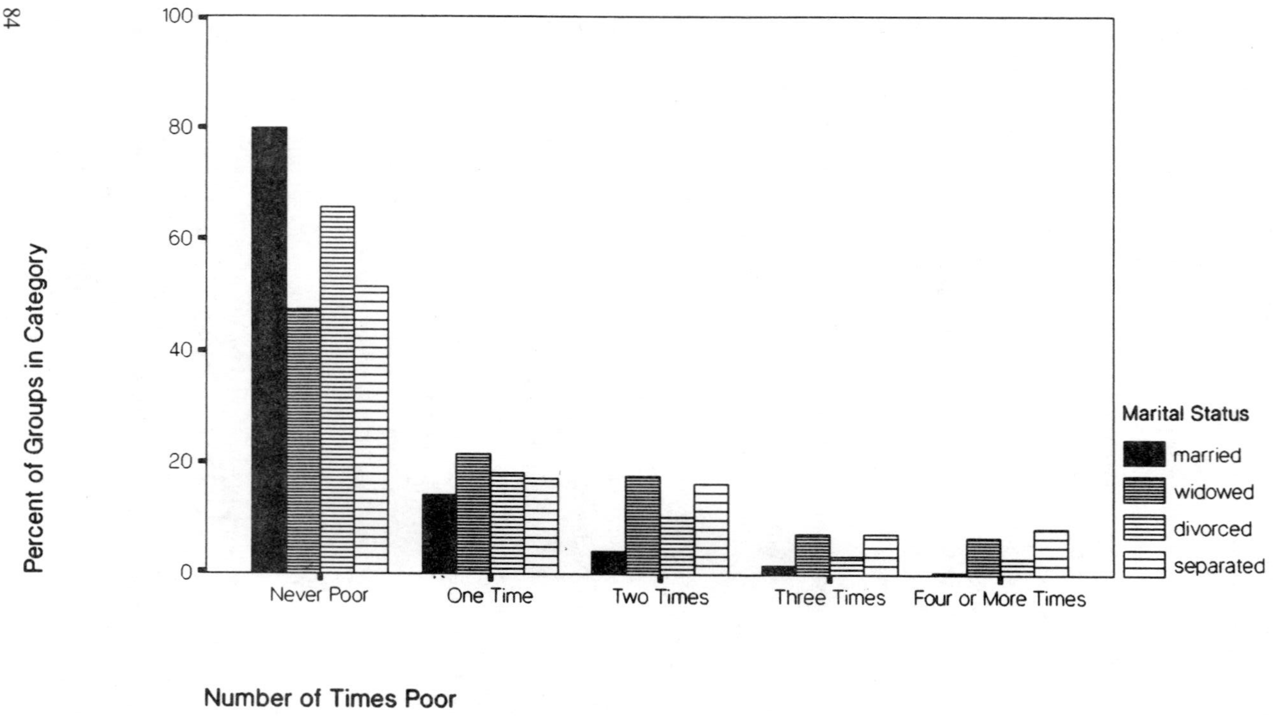

Figure 4.4. Number of Times Poor by Marital Status

same number of opportunities as the widowed, for example, to evidence poverty in an NLS interview. Poverty figures, when recalculated on the basis of the number of respondent-interviews (i.e., taking into account differences in attrition) reveal that the actual risks of poverty are highest for the separated (33.0% of all interviews with separated responderts over time found them to be poor), followed closely by the widowed (29.9%). The divorced are substantially lower, with 15% of their respondent-interview contacts falling into the poverty range, while the rate for the married was a strikingly low 5.4%.

These comparisons, then, confirm the pattern which has been emerging from the very beginning, of differential economic risks. Widowed and separated women appear to have greater risks of poverty than the divorced, who themselves face higher odds than the women who remain in marriages. Because the women who are separated and widowed started with lower average incomes, the decrease at the end of marriage is more likely to propel them below the threshold for poverty. The divorcing women, in contrast, may have larger income reduction and still escape the label of poverty.

Overall, episodes of poverty are quite common among midlife women after their marriages end. For most women, poverty is not a persistent condition, but many remain "near poor" and few see a return to substantial income levels relative to needs.

CHANGING SOURCES OF INCOME

The end of a marriage involves not only a change in the amount of income received by midlife women and their families, but also a shift in the sources from which income is derived. Loss of the husband's contribution is counterbalanced to some extent by new sources, such as child support, Social Security benefits to widows and children of covered workers, and in some cases enhanced earnings by the formerly married woman. In addition, any who qualify based on need may turn to public supports such as AFDC, food stamps, or public assistance.

Four general categories of income are examined here. The first is income generated by the respondent through her own employment, or employment-related benefits (i.e., unemployment, Social Security, or other disability payments). The second category includes the income provided by the present/former/late spouse, from earnings, a family farm, business, or through employment benefits.[3] The third category is composed of transfer income from public sources, including Social Security survivor benefits, food stamps, and welfare or AFDC. Finally, there is an "other" category, covering wages

Table 4.3 Percentage of Income Coming from Various Sources Over Time by Marital Category

| | *Interview Time Period* | | | | | |
	0	1	2	3	4	5
Married						
Respondent[a]	17.8	18.5	18.3	18.4	18.7	19.3
Husband	62.5	61.0	60.6	59.9	58.3	56.8
Other	19.1	19.9	20.5	21.2	22.5	23.5
Transfers	.6	.6	.6	.6	.4	.4
Widowed						
Respondent	25.0	46.5	43.5	50.4	46.0	50.9
Husband	46.7	2.1	1.3	.6	.2	.4
Other	26.0	41.9	39.5	36.2	47.7	33.9
Transfers	2.3	9.5	15.7	12.8	6.0	14.8
Divorced						
Respondent	33.1	67.7	68.9	67.8	74.3	72.4
Husband	48.4	13.9	12.7	11.1	7.9	5.9
Other	16.5	13.2	13.9	15.3	12.0	17.7
Transfers	2.0	5.3	4.6	5.7	5.7	4.0
Separated						
Respondent	34.8	60.4	52.8	50.7	50.4	38.3
Husband	42.1	8.3	8.6	6.7	3.7	1.3
Other	17.8	18.3	18.7	14.3	13.7	16.4
Transfers	5.3	12.9	20.0	28.3	32.3	44.0

a. Additional detail on how these categories were created is available in Note 4 in this chapter.

and income from family members in the household, rental or dividend income, child support, alimony, annuities, and income from any other source not specified. Table 4.3 profiles the changing composition of income for women experiencing departures from marriage. Figures are based on the percentage of aggregate income derived from each of the four categories. Although the percentages add up to 100 (within minor rounding error), it must be recalled that the "size of the pie" being divided up for widowed, separated, and divorced women is markedly reduced at the point when their marriages end. It is not that income from a particular source, for example earnings of the woman, increases so dramatically as the fact that those dollars become more important as a component of the new (and smaller) household income.

Among the married there is only minor and gradual change in sources of income, with the respondents increasing slightly their contributions over time, a corresponding small decline in contributions by husbands, and a growth in the "other" category. In contrast, all three transitional groups display dramatic declines in the percentage of income from the husband from Time1 onward—but the changes go well beyond this shift. For widows the husband drops from about 47% of total income to 2% or less. In effect, the great majority of widows received no income from the deceased husband, but a few (4%-8%) continued to receive resources, such as income from a business, following his death. Correspondingly, the percentage of overall income generated by the widow from her own employment or work-related benefits increased from 25% of all income to 43%-50%.

Another major shift is in transfer income, which includes survivor benefits from Social Security. These benefits jump from 2% in Time0 to a high of nearly 16% of total income coming to these households. "Other" income sources, including annuities or earnings of children, also become a much more important part of household income for widows after their husbands die.

Among the divorced there is a substantially different picture. Neither transfer income nor income from the "other" sources constitutes a notably increased component of aggregate income in postmarital interviews. Instead, the major adaptation in sources among midlife divorcees is the dramatically increased importance of the women's earnings (and employment-related benefits). These move from one third of aggregate income to levels between two thirds and three fourths of the total following divorce. The husbands' contributions diminish significantly, but still benefit many households to a lesser degree.

If we contrast those cases in which women move directly from married to divorced status with women who had first separated, an even more distinct picture emerges. Women who had separated prior to divorce had already made their adjustment in terms of sources of income, so they saw relatively little additional change at divorce. Among "direct divorcers" husbands had contributed over half (57.6%) of the income at Time0, with wives contributing much less (26.6%). Those women who moved directly to divorce, however, very quickly caught up with their previously separated peers, so that few differences remained between the groups shortly after divorce. There were two exceptions in that divorced women who had previously been separated continued to receive more income from transfers (AFDC, food stamps) and less from their own earnings in some subsequent years.

Finally, in the separated group the contribution from earnings of the woman also jumps abruptly as the marriage ends, and that of the husband shrinks. Noteworthy in the data for the separated is the fact that husbands contributed less in the final interview during marriages than in any other

Table 4.4 Proportions Receiving and Median Amount Received from Child
Support and Alimony Among Divorced and from Social Security
Among Widowed Women

	Interview Time Period				
	1	*2*	*3*	*4*	*5*
Widows: Social Security[a]					
% Receiving Income	36.6%[b]	44.5%	47.9%	32.1%	40.3%
Median Amount	$2,464	$4,473	$4,179	$3,994	$4,074
Divorce: Alimony and Child Support					
% Receiving Income	36.9%	37.9%	33.1%	30.6%	25.3%
Median Amount	$3,831	$3,317	$3,096	$2,535	$2,396

a. Social Security other than disability.
b. There were high percentages of widowed respondents with missing data on these questions because they
were asked separately in only five of nine interviews. The findings represent the percentages and median
amounts for those responding on specific questions about Social Security income.

group. This corresponds with the picture of these households as financially
disadvantaged, with an economic disruption among the possible cause of
dissolution. There is a significant and linear increase in the reliance on
transfer income (e.g., AFDC and welfare) among the separated with the
passage of time. This may reflect the inadequacy of support from husbands,
limited earning capacity of the women, or the increasingly selective character
of the group over time. As some women move forward to divorce or
reconciliation, those who remain see their collective reliance on income from
food stamps, AFDC, and other welfare-based programs grow.

Social Security and Child Support/Alimony

Although the previous breakdown provides a general notion of
the shifting sources of income for women after marriage, further examination
of the specific roles of survivor benefits from Social Security and child
support and alimony is warranted. These programs are designed to provide
income replacement or to serve as a "safety net" for formerly married women
with dependent children. What proportion of women report receiving such
income after divorce or widowhood? What amounts are reported and are the
amounts substantial? Table 4.4 outlines the proportion of widowed and
divorced women receiving income from each of these sources over time and
the median dollar amounts corrected for inflation among those receiving such
income.[4]

Fewer than half of the responding widows reported getting benefits from Social Security in each of the interviews after their spouses died. Their only eligibility for such benefits was by virtue of having dependent children at home and meeting the earnings test. Because 23.3% said they had no dependent children just after widowhood, and an additional group (23.3%) with missing values undoubtedly were predominated by childless widows, this low rate is not altogether inappropriate.

As a percentage of the median income for this group over time, figures ranged from a low of 23% of the total in Time1 to 32%-39% in the subsequent four measurements. Although not replacing the husband's contribution, amounts of this size could constitute an important component of total income for many households. Yet widows receiving benefits from Social Security were neither more nor less likely than their peers not receiving such benefits to be poor at any interview after their husbands died.

For the divorced between about 25% and 38% reported receiving income from child support and/or alimony. Although the dollar amounts cannot be separated, the bulk of this income is probably child support rather than spousal support or alimony. The dollar amounts here are somewhat lower than for those to widows from Social Security. Again receipt of these payments was unrelated to the likelihood of poverty for a divorced woman. Neither form of payment approached replacement of the income contribution lost from the husband.

VARIATIONS BY SOCIAL
AND DEMOGRAPHIC TRAITS

The evidence from NLS midlife women confirms declines in income and increases in rates of poverty, with little improvement over time for those who remain widowed, separated, or divorced. The question remaining is whether it is the marital transition, the characteristics of the women, or both that determine their outcomes relative to income and poverty. One way of examining this question is to use factors shown by previous research to influence economic well-being among midlife women. By drawing comparisons among women we can then examine whether such diversity is really responsible for most changes in their economic status. Table 4.5 presents sociodemographic comparisons for only those midlife women whose marriages ended. Caution must be used in evaluation of the results in later years, because the number in each category shrinks over time, and some groups become quite small. Three items are compared for each of the groups: total family income, average percentage change from Time0 income levels, and

Table 4.5 Median Total Family Income, Median Percentage Decline in Income, and Percentage Poor Before, and Five Measurements After, Marital Termination, by Selected Characteristics for Women Whose Marriages Ended

	Interview Time Period					
	0	1	2	3	4	5
Race						
Black (*N*)	252	255	219	176	139	107
Income($)	13,594	11,242	9,025	9,521	9,800	9,261
% Decline	—	23	32	28	29	28
% Poor	38	41	51	48	48	53
White (*N*)	492	500	387	287	203	155
Income($)	23,935	12,915	14,317	13,137	14,633	13,941
% Decline	—	35	39	38	37	35
% Poor	13	17	22	20	17	17
Education						
Less than High School						
N	356	356	291	223	165	136
Income($)	14,289	9,712	7,943	8,556	8,492	8,114
% Decline	—	32	35	38	31	31
% Poor	33	43	49	47	48	50
High School						
N	285	290	228	176	125	88
Income($)	24,116	13,132	15,110	14,054	15,603	14,794
% Decline	—	35	39	34	37	34
% Poor	12	20	19	17	18	13
Beyond High School						
N	102	107	86	63	51	37
Income($)	34,079	22,836	19,897	20,290	20,109	21,800
% Decline	—	28	36	30	34	30
% Poor	5	11	11	8	12	0
Age						
30-39 *(N)*	202	200	162	135	110	93
Income($)	20,100	13,563	14,047	12,781	13,566	14,326
% Decline	—	30	31	21	28	27
% Poor	21	26	29	20	26	32
40-49 *(N)*	403	423	348	276	213	155
Income($)	20,639	12,142	12,425	11,186	11,700	10,706
% Decline	—	33	38	41	34	34
% Poor	18	28	31	28	25	27
50-59 *(N)*	132	132	96	52	19	14
Income($)	16,453	9,662	7,672	5,719	6,930	8,382
% Decline	—	37	46	56	44	50
% Poor	21	37	36	52	46	47

Table 4.5 Continued

			Interview Time Period			
	0	1	2	3	4	5
Employment						
Employed (N)	448	447	348	259	185	153
Income($)	21,309	14,025	13,854	12,861	14,633	13,500
% Decline	—	29	38	37	38	31
% Poor	16	19	20	20	21	19
Not Employed (N)	246	242	198	152	113	99
Income($)	16,754	8,309	7,694	8,727	9,824	9,125
% Decline	—	40	38	35	28	34
% Poor	32	51	55	50	46	49
Children						
None (N)	70	68	45	9	9	8
Income($)	13,971	8,620	6,324	8,556	9,824	7,435
% Decline	—	38	46	18	38	39
% Poor	11	25	30	33	33	26
1-2 (N)	190	187	141	95	78	70
Income($)	22,091	13,303	13,025	13,098	15,372	12,968
% Decline	—	35	43	40	34	37
% Poor	17	22	25	20	20	24
3 or more (N)	191	191	164	127	106	85
Income($)	17,971	12,256	13,801	12,324	13,322	12,589
% Decline	—	24	25	23	17	14
% Poor	37	46	41	42	36	39
Income Level						
Top 1/3 (N)	283	272	219	158	113	78
Income($)	35,316	18,504	17,318	17,485	17,574	18,150
% Decline	—	51	57	53	53	51
% Poor	0	10	13	10	10	9
Bottom1/3 (N)	214	198	155	122	91	74
Income($)	7,828	7,835	7,283	7,187	7,474	8,342
% Decline	—	−1.1	−11	−3	−14	−16
% Poor	65	56	53	55	54	53

the percentage poor at each interview. As the results show, there is considerable consistency with prior research and within groups for these three indicators of economic standing.

On income and rates of poverty white women fare better than do black. Income contrasts by race are dramatically reduced, however, when marriage ends, after which both groups show persistent income levels for the next 7-8 years. White women also experience slightly greater percentage declines

(35%-38% vs. 23%-32% among black women) from their income levels during the final year of marriage.

Education makes more of a difference on some indicators than others. There is a clear relationship between income and education level both before and after marriages end, with more educated women reporting higher incomes. The mirror relationship holds for poverty, such that with higher educational attainment the risks of poverty are lower. There is little relationship, however, between the percentage decline in income and education. It appears from these results that education, as a preexisting human capital factor, helps to shape income both during and after marriage. Its effects remain relatively consistent across all three education categories as the women move out of marriage.

With regard to age at the end of marriage, older women (50-59) had lower incomes both during and after marriage than their younger counterparts. They also experienced slightly sharper declines in total income and higher rates of poverty.

Women who were working just prior to their separations, widowhoods, or divorces experienced very little change in poverty rates after the end of marriage, compared to a 20% increase among women who had not been employed. The employed women also had lower percentage decreases in income and higher incomes both before and after their marriages ended.

As Table 4.5 shows, midlife women with large families fared somewhat worse in terms of poverty than those with smaller families, both before and after their marriages ended. Childless women, however, had the lowest incomes and saw larger declines in their incomes over time than did the midlife women from larger households.

Finally, the outcomes vary considerably depending on whether the women started in the top or bottom one third of the income distribution in Time0. Women with the highest incomes continued fairly high income levels after their marriages ended, but at the same time experienced the largest relative declines from Time0. Reducing from a very high to a modest income level, however, throws very few of these women into poverty after marriage. In contrast, the majority of women who were in the bottom one third of the income distribution prior to separation, widowhood or divorce were in poverty at Time0. Ironically, the ending of her marriage involved little or no economic penalty for the average woman in this poorest group. Rates of poverty actually decline about 10%, probably because of a reduced level of need, and incomes for the majority of women improved somewhat, as indicated by the negative median percentage decline in income figures for this group. In the case of these women, the loss of the husband reduces demand for income, and it appears that other sources, including supports from public programs such as AFDC or Social Security, may contribute to some improvement in income.

These contrasts aside, key patterns in Table 4.5 are consistent with the findings by marital status. The women, regardless of their characteristics or varied economic "starting points" experience an income loss when marriage ends, followed by a fluctuating but fairly flat progression for the subsequent four interviews. Rates of poverty generally increase, and remain elevated as long as women remain in their formerly married statuses. It appears that, instead of shaping posttransition changes in divergent ways, the characteristics in Table 4.5 influence the economic standing of women as they approach the end of marriage, and thus their relative well-being afterward. The economic disadvantage associated with departure from marriage, therefore, appears to be rather equitably spread across all categories of women.

The differential association of these traits with widowhood, separation, and divorce suggests that some or most of the differences between these groups may be accounted for by the traits of the woman, rather than the type of marital transition she experiences. In order to examine this possibility further, several hierarchical multiple regression models were evaluated. In these analyses the variables in Table 4.5 (in their continuous form for age, education, and number of children) are entered followed by dummy variables for the marital statuses of separated, widowed, or divorced. This is to determine whether, beyond the explanatory power of these sociodemographic traits, marital status makes any added difference in economic outcomes. Three dependent variables (percentage of income decline for each respondent 5 years after marital transition, income relative to needs in Time1 and in Time5) are used.[5]

Results in Table 4.6 demonstrate that once other traits have been taken into account, being separated, widowed, or divorced makes no significant difference in these three outcomes. In the model for percentage income decline in the fifth year after marital transitions, only being in the bottom one third of the income distribution before marital termination and being a worker made a significant difference, both diminishing the amount of that decline. The overall explanatory power of this model (the R^2) is small, explaining only 17.5% of the variation in income change from the Time0 interview. The three marital status variables added only 1.4% to the explained variance.

Results for income-to-needs ratios in Time1 and Time5 are somewhat distinct. In both years, having had a high income during marriage (being in the top one third of incomes in Time0) and having been employed at the end of marriage enhanced income relative to needs. Short-term income-to-needs

Table 4.6 Results of Hierarchical Multiple Regressions on Five Year Income Decline and Income to Needs Ratios in Time1 and Time5

| Dependent | Decline | | Income to Needs Ratios | | | |
| | | | Time1 | | Time5 | |
Indepedent	B	Beta	B	Beta	B	Beta
Bottom 1/3 of Income	−107.2	−.428***				
Top 1/3 of Income			.970	.233***	.559	.137*
Work in Time0	−37.6	−.160*	.526	.129*	.689	.172**
Years of Education			.149	.219**	.209	.315***
Number of Children in Time0			−.142	−.159*		
Race (Black = 1)					−.921	−.231***
Widowed	−18.7	−.080	−.064	−.015	.120	.030
Divorced	−20.5	−.089	−.094	−.023	.267	.068
Separated	12.8	.053	−.481	−.115	.114	.028
R^2	.175		.267		.350	
Increment to R^2	.014		.011		.003	

*$p < .05$; **$p < .01$; ***$p < .001$

ratios, however, are influenced negatively by a larger number of children in the household, while long-term economic well-being is negatively influenced for women who are black. These regressions for income to needs in Time1 and Time5 hold more explanatory power (i.e., R^2 is .267 and .350, respectively), but the variables for marital status transitions again add little or nothing.

SUMMARY AND IMPLICATIONS: CHANGES IN ECONOMIC STANDING

To a great extent, the data on changes in economic status of the NLS mature women confirmed expectations regarding loss of economic protection at the end of marriage. All three transitional groups experienced significant declines in total family income. These lowered levels of income were sustained over time, suggesting an absence of substantial recovery of income as long as the women remained outside the boundaries of marriage. In a subsequent chapter on remarriage, the important question of whether remarriage results in improved economic well-being will be addressed.

Also important, however, is the fact that midlife women whose marriages were about to end had lower average incomes than their peers who would remain married. For one subgroup of the divorced, this lower income level was the result of the prior separation, with its correspondingly lowered income levels, prior to a final legal dissolution. In fact, it was apparent on income and poverty measures that the point of separation was the major financial turning point for women who subsequently went on to divorce. Although there was a much smaller and sometimes positive change in economic status for divorcees following separation, divorce made no major difference in terms of income or poverty for these women. Women who moved directly from marriage to divorce, however, showed clear and sudden changes in conjunction with dissolution of their marriage.

For the widowed and separated groups there were not such obvious precursors to lower family income. Among the widowed, few women had reported illness among their husbands that might have limited his ability to work. For separated women the composition of the group, including many less educated women and more black women, probably translated into couple traits providing lower (and less secure) incomes even during marriage. Both divorcing and separating women may have had lower incomes in marriage due to economic stressors (e.g., unemployment, business failure, etc.) that might also have contributed to the breakup of the marital relationship. Even with longitudinal data it is difficult to separate out what appear to be long and complex chains of causation, often going back many years prior to the ending of the marriage.

Important, too, is the finding that the characteristics of the women, not the manner in which their marriages ended, substantially influenced their economic consequences. To a large extent the diversity in economic fortunes seen when we compare widowed, separated, and divorced women is related to the social and demographic traits (e.g., education, race, number of children, employment, prior income) that vary among the groups. The separated, who had the lowest incomes during marriage, a very high proportion black, low education, and larger numbers of children, fared the most poorly on most indices of economic well-being when their marriages ended. The fact that they became separated (as opposed to being widowed, for example) may be less salient than the configuration of characteristics they bring to their marital transition. Although those who had the highest incomes lost the most in a proportional sense, they still maintained higher economic well-being and lower rates of poverty than women who had ended their marriages in very marginal or poverty-level circumstances.

Poverty was itself a fairly common outcome among those who became widowed, separated, or divorced, especially among the separated. Also telling are the significant numbers in all marital groups who are very close to the poverty threshold (i.e., in the *Marginal* income group). Not only do rates of poverty, per se, rise after marriage ends for women, but there are also substantial numbers of women whose households balance on the brink of poverty, and poverty status is quite dynamic. Other research (Bane & Ellwood, 1986) shows that the longer one remains in poverty the lower the chances for escape. This paints a fairly bleak picture for the most disadvantaged women among the formerly married.

Of course there remain some qualifications and limitations. These data suffer from "right censoring," that is an inability to tell what happened after individuals ended their participation in the sample or the study ended (Berk, 1983). Sample sizes become too small to draw definitive conclusions over time. And, because the age range is limited, the dynamics of changes may also be very different for younger divorcees and older widows.

One notable subgroup within the sample was those in the lowest one third for pretransition income. They differed from the overall pattern of change after marriage, with income levels remaining constant and poverty rates declining slightly. Perhaps the old line that says "When you've got nothing you've got nothing to lose," applies here. The so-called safety net programs are undoubtedly contributing to many of these poorest households both during and after marriage. The departure or loss of a spouse in such cases may have limited impact except to lower the number of mouths to feed. This diversity both across sociodemographic groups and within the ranks of the separated, widowed, and divorced reinforces the fact that most marital groups had a mixture of income levels and economic outcomes among their numbers. Not all of the separated were poor nor were all of the divorcing women relatively advantaged. These important traits appear to make more difference in how women fare financially than the manner in which their marriages end.

Thus to a large extent economic consequences following the departure from marriage depend on characteristics and decisions that had shaped the woman's life long before her marriage ended. What can we conclude about the economic protection of marriage? Undoubtedly the majority of women whose marriages ended experienced a decline in their economic well-being, primarily due to the loss of the income provided by husbands. Widowed women on average experienced about a 35% decline in income, the divorced a 39% loss, and the separated 23% lower levels of household income. This lost income of husbands was not substantially replaced either through social programs, such as Social Security and AFDC, or through supports from the former husbands. Even if the husband continued to contribute through alimony or child support, that contribution in no way compared to his prior financial support to the household. Women were left with their own earnings, some benefits, and could resort to AFDC and food stamps if they were eligible.

The decisions made by women after marriage can also influence their long-term income prospects. In the next two chapters we examine further the roles of labor force participation and remarriage as adaptive responses to loss of economic protection at divorce, separation, and widowhood.

NOTES

1. This definition leaves open the possibility that some households include parents of the respondent or other kin who could in turn contribute to the economic resources of the household. There is no consistent way of excluding such cases, but examination of the data suggests that relatively few households exist in the total NLS sample where the respondent is other than the head of household or spouse of head. Further, in cases where other kin are present, their contribution to the income of the household is considered to be a realistic factor, valid for inclusion. Due to limitations in the gathering of income information, which may underestimate the income of women experiencing marital transitions (especially widows), the income figures for the first year are corrected (see Holden et al., 1986). When husbands died or departed part of the way through the year, their income was not asked about in the subsequent interview. An estimation procedure added the number of months' income (based on the prior interview's contribution from the husband) to the family income for this first year to correct for this oversight, which would otherwise make Time 1 income artificially low. Keep in mind that all income values here have been corrected for inflation to equivalency in 1981 dollars.

2. In order to evaluate the scope of differences between those women who completed the five posttransitional interviews and those who did not, the widowed, divorced, and separated groups were divided into two subgroups. One participated for the five postmarital interviews, although women in the other had been lost for various reasons. The comparisons were drawn on income before the marriage ended, ratio of income to needs in the first posttransition interview, number of dependent children in the home, age when marriage ended, employment status at the first measurement after marriage, and years of education completed. Here only differences that achieved statistical significance are reported.

Among the widowed group, those who left ($N = 233$) had fewer children at home ($F = 10.4$, $p = .001$) and were older ($M = 46$ vs. $M = 35$, $F = 54.3$, $p = .0000$) at widowhood.

For the divorced group, those who did not complete the five measurements ($N = 171$) were less educated ($F = 3.97$, $p = .047$), and older ($M = 41$ vs. $M = 37$, $F = 6.18$, $p = .013$) when their marriages ended.

The largest number of differences appear for the separated, who were the most dynamic group in terms of ways not to complete the five surveys within this subsample (i.e., reconciliation, divorce, sample attrition, or being separated after 1976). For this group those who did not complete the five interviews ($N = 227$) had higher incomes during marriage ($M = \$19,393$ vs. $M = \$13,276$, $F = 4.82$, $p = .029$), had fewer children ($F = 5.47$, $p = .02$), had higher income to needs ratios right after separation ($F = 11.09$, $p = .001$), were more educated ($F = 4.47$, $p = .035$), were older ($F = 33.4$, $p = .000$), and were more white ($\chi^2 = 24.25$, $p = .00001$). Most of these characteristics appear to be consistent with Cherlin's (1981) discussion, which argued that many women who remained separated did so because divorce was too expensive or inaccessible. The characteristics of those who left the sample suggest that less advantaged women, most concentrated among black respondents, remained in the ranks of the separated over time.

3. For conceptual reasons, it was important to discern the relative contributions of husband and wife to the overall household income as marriages ended. Women's earnings and benefits were asked about in a clear fashion because they are the focus of the study. Income for other household members was asked in different ways over time, however, so that combinations to create consistency could only be made with some concessions. For example, in some of the years funds from a business or profession, pension, or other benefits were listed separately for respondent, husband, and other family members. In other years only the respondent and others were separated. Income from these sources was important to a minority of households, but could be an important component in those households. The assumption is that, because most households contained no adults other than husband and wife, a majority of businesses would be those of husbands. Income from a business or profession, from a farm, and from other work-related benefits (e.g., disability income to someone in the household other than the respondent) is assigned as the husband's throughout, even though in some cases this may overestimate his income contribution. These problems plague all groups of women equally, and should not bias the comparative results. Although it would have been desirable to place child support and alimony as part of the husband's ongoing contribution in households of the separated or divorced, the lumping together of this income within the "other" category in several of the years made this distinction impossible.

4. It was simple to separate out child support and alimony in the last four data collections, when they were asked about in a distinct question. In the first five surveys under consideration here (1967 data were not employed), alimony and child support were lumped with annuities and any "other" income not already cited by the respondent. The prior income questions had been so detailed in most cases, however, that there would have been little other than annuities to include in this category with the income of interest here. Using this category to represent alimony and child support may, however, overestimate the amounts received and should be interpreted cautiously.

For Social Security income other than disability, the question was included in five surveys, and in four others was lumped into an "other" category, from which it was irretrievable. This is because a number of other income sources were also included within that "other" range, making the amount a poor estimator of Social Security benefits. Fairly high levels of missing data are the result. Since these questions asked about Social Security payments other than disability, it is possible to have included retirement benefits. Because these women were not old enough to receive retirement benefits in their own right, and almost none had husbands old enough to do so, it is improbable that retirement benefits constituted a notable portion of the income reported here.

5. Obviously there are a variety of potential dependent variables that could be used for such regression analyses. These were chosen to represent both diversity in time relative to the end of marriage and to show two different approaches to economic status. Income-to-needs measures reflect a measure comparable across more diverse groups, while the percentage decline reflects the NLS respondent's position relative to her economic status in marriage.

5

The End of Marriage
and Changing
Employment

New or increased involvement in the labor force is an important change in the lives of many midlife women experiencing the ending of marriage (Kitson with Holmes, in press). Some authors suggest that it serves as a means of adapting both socially and economically after marriage ends (Lopata, 1973). Socially it may provide a new role identity, social interaction, or self-esteem. In economic terms, work provides essential income and benefits such as health insurance to the midlife woman and her dependents. The focus in this chapter is twofold: the effect of marital termination on working, and changes from work to economic well-being.

As we have already seen, women become heavily reliant on their earnings, which constitute a significant proportion of their reduced household incomes after widowhood, divorce, or separation (for further details see Chapter 4). Other research has confirmed that many women who had been homemakers are forced to move into the labor force, primarily by the need for additional income (Kitson with Holmes, in press; Shaw, 1983). One study of female-headed households reported that 33% of those that were poor had managed to escape poverty through the income from the women's employment (Bane & Ellwood, 1986). Determining causation is problematic in these cases, however, because expected income may shape work decisions, and certainly work decisions influence income. As we saw in Chapter 3, women whose marriages would end varied as to the percentage working at the interview just prior to the termination of their marriages. Women in both the divorcing and separating groups had significantly higher percentages employed (17% and 11% higher than married women, respectively), while the widowed were only slightly higher in their level of involvement. All four marital groups held fairly positive attitudes toward employment, even women who did not have jobs at the time. It should be recalled that any labor force adaptations by the formerly married women in the sample were occurring within a larger framework of dramatic change. During the time of the study the rates of employment among women increased generally and attitudes toward employment by women grew more favorable (Bianchi & Spain, 1986). Given this dynamic background for labor force changes, it remains essential to observe any changes in behaviors of the continuously married women as a baseline.

DIMENSIONS OF
LABOR FORCE INVOLVEMENT

Research on women's changing employment patterns during this time period has suggested that a variety of factors, including marital status, shape decisions individual women make as to whether or not to work. The ending of marriage may be a key turning point, because it significantly alters more than one element contributing to these decisions (Peterson, 1989). Both the removal of possible spousal opposition and the probable decrease of household income create new circumstances. Both are thought generally to promote working, even among women who are unenthusiastic about employment or unable to locate high quality jobs. There are several ways in which women change their labor force behavior in response to the end of marriage. The first option generally considered is that of seeking work by women who had been homemakers. A second option, for those already employed, is to increase their hours of work in the current job or to change jobs. Third, women may upgrade their occupations, either through added training, job change, or more vigorous pursuit of career advancement in the current job. All three of these adaptations should serve to improve their income generated by employment coming into the household.

Less consideration has been given to another type of adaptation in labor force behavior; reduced working hours or withdrawal from the labor force after the end of marriage. Scenarios in which a wife might have worked to provide income or health insurance for a spouse in failing health or in which income supports, such as Social Security or child support, actually improve a household's financial situation after termination of the marriage, are seldom included in labor force discussions. One earlier study found that there were nearly equivalent rates of entry into and departure from employment and increase or reduction in hours following death of spouse among older widows (Morgan, 1984). Analyses of changes in labor force participation must, therefore, include movement either into or out of employment as possible avenues of adaptation to marital endings for women.

Work and Economic Issues: Widows Versus Divorced Women

The context in which decisions regarding labor force participation are made differ in important ways for widowed and divorced women. These differences originate with the distinct policies designed to provide income support to each of these groups. Childless women, who are not affected by these program provisions, make their decisions based on factors influencing all women workers (e.g., education, attitudes toward employment, and the opportunities available to them for well-paying jobs, etc.). Social Security survivor benefits, for which many widowed mothers in midlife are eligible, are subject (as are all benefits of this program) to an earnings test. In 1988, for example, benefits were reduced by one dollar for each two dollars earned in wages above $6,120.[1] This reduces the income incentive for working in that it limits the benefit amount from Social Security to women with substantial earnings (Lopata & Brehm, 1986). Instead of serving as an earnings supplement to replace lost wages of the husband, Social Security was designed as a safety net program to provide basic income support, especially for those widows undertaking full-time child care activities.

Although there are no comparable income support programs designed specifically for divorced women, moderate to high earnings may still reduce income from some sources. For example, a former wife's current or potential earnings may help a judge to determine whether she is awarded spousal support (Weitzman, 1985). And even though child support is ostensibly independent of the ex-wife's earning level, in all likelihood award amounts are reduced by the perceived capacity of a custodial mother to support her children through her own employment (McLindon, 1987). For both widowhood and divorce, then, the outcome is the same. The ability of a formerly married woman to be self-supporting via earnings reduces the other income support she is likely to receive. The attractiveness of increased labor force activity may be dampened by the penalties on earnings imposed by these policies. For some women, especially those able to command only modest salaries, these reductions in income support may serve as serious disincentives to entering the labor force altogether.

But how does the ending of marriage shape involvement in paid employment? Do large numbers of formerly married women enter (or reenter) the working world? Are there systematic differences between widowed, separated, and divorced women in these behaviors? How quickly do these changes occur? Are differences between the marital categories associated with other traits (e.g., race, educational background, presence of dependent children, age)? Is employment an effective means of escaping from poverty or improving economic well-being for formerly married women? These are the primary questions addressed in this chapter.

Changes Prior to
the Termination of Marriage

For some women changes in involvement with the labor force may begin well in advance of marital termination (Peterson, 1989). Some examples might better illustrate this point. Suppose a midlife woman, employed full-time, learns that her husband has a serious illness that will result in his death. She may choose to quit her job, rather than hiring a nurse, in order to care for him. This woman might return to employment following the death of her spouse, both for needed income and because it was her typical pattern of behavior. In contrast, a nonworking wife concerned about the possible breakup of her marriage may seek employment or training even before the issues of separation or divorce are discussed with her husband. In such fashion labor force adaptation may begin, or be confounded by, events much earlier than the official or recognized ending of the marriage. For these reasons it is especially critical to take a long-range view of employment activities. Examining such long-range behavioral change is complicated by the fact that an array of forces unrelated to marital status is simultaneously influencing women's decisions to enter or exit the labor force. These include bearing and caring for children, shifting income amounts or needs within the family (e.g., unemployment of the husband), illness of family members, and the nature of employment opportunities for women, among others. Beyond these factors, traits of the woman and her human capital shape the costs and benefits of choosing to work under a given set of familial and societal conditions.

Given the multiplicity of forces shaping employment decisions of midlife women, drawing causal linkages between these changes and departure from marriage is necessarily limited. We cannot know whether it is the need for additional income or other factors that led a particular formerly married woman to move toward the labor force. The married comparison group helps to place the changes of the formerly married in context, however, because most of the other forces influencing labor force decisions affect married and formerly married women more or less equally. Selected comparisons presented here, by stretching back several years prior to marital transitions, shed additional light on the extent of labor force changes before marriage ends.

LABOR FORCE
PARTICIPATION RATES

Figure 5.1 describes the changes over time in labor force participation, as reported by the midlife women in the NLS panel. In this case the time frame has been extended back to four measurements prior to termination,[2] so that more past behavior can serve as a basis for evaluation of trends. As was seen with the income and poverty comparisons in Chapter 4, however, the more removed in time any interview is from Time0 and Time1, the fewer respondents are available to establish trends confidently. Figure 5.1 shows the percentage of respondents in each marital category who were in the labor force (as it is traditionally defined, including those currently working, with a job but not at work, or looking for work in the survey week) across a nine-interview span.[3] Remaining activities not presented include full-time homemaking, which was the second most common choice in all groups and times, and a range of other activities (seeking education, unable to work due to health, retired, never worked, other) selected by only a small percentage of any sample group in each interview.

First, responses of the married comparison group indicate a gradual increase in labor force participation over time, especially in the final three interviews. This increase may reflect the entry or return to employment of women completing childbearing or parenting of preschoolers, response to an increasing need for income as children grow, changing attitudes toward and opportunities for women's employment, or some combination of these and other factors. There is a corresponding decline in the proportion of married women who are keeping house, but little change in the "other" category over time. For the married group "Time0" dates were randomly selected and thus should minimize systematic trends related to historical or economic events (e.g., recessions or low rates of unemployment) affecting everyone in the labor force.

Hidden behind the figures for the married, however, are some important differences between black and white women. In all of the years up to Time3 there were significant differences by race, with black married women initially having 20% more of their numbers in the labor force in Time–3 than was the

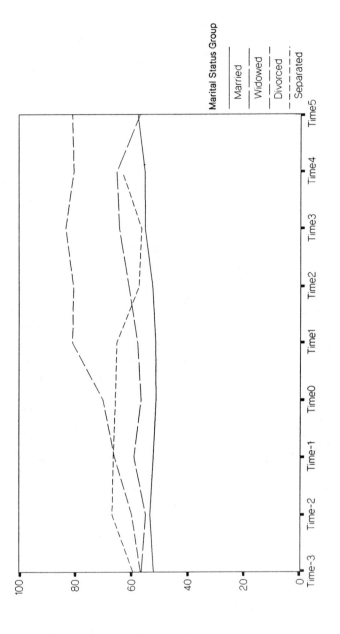

Figure 5.1. Labor Force Participation Rates by Marital Status Groups Over Time

case for whites. These differences diminish over time, so that by Time5 the difference between the two groups was a slight 2.5%.

Turning to the widowed there is a mixed picture. Prior to death of the spouse labor force rates fluctuated at a level slightly higher than that of the married comparison group. Once widowhood occurs rates increase slightly, to a high of 65.2% about 6-7 years later. Perhaps surprising after discussing the married, there is no significant difference by race among the widowed group in any year, with differences by race ranging from 2.5% up to 12.5%.[4] As with the married, the primary counter-balancing decrease in all three transitional groups is from those keeping house. Among widows, however, the final interview also showed growth in the "other" category, with some increase in the widows labeling themselves retired or "unable to work."

These data do not show large numbers of NLS widows moving into the labor force in response to the deaths of their husbands. For widows in this age range, other constraints, available income supports, or lack of desire to participate in paid employment appear to limit any major increases in working associated with movement into widowhood. Alternatively, similar numbers of widows may be withdrawing from the labor force, leaving rates of participation relatively unchanged, a possibility addressed later. Because a majority of widows are already workers well in advance of the death of their spouses, most of those remaining may be disinclined toward employment or lack the human capital to command substantial wages. In general, even after loss of their husbands the widows do not participate much more than the married women in the labor force.

The labor force story for the divorced greatly differs from that of the widows. Although both groups have similar initial rates of labor force activity, the divorced group steadily increases its involvement, years in advance of the dissolution of marriage. Thus a large and growing segment of the divorced women are already involved in employment at the legal end of their marriages. Even so, they experience a substantial (10.8%) increase in labor force activity by the interview immediately following divorce. Although there are no significant differences in labor force rates by race except in the first interview (Time–3), this immediate postdivorce jump is largely the result of movement by white women into the labor force. After this initial increase, however, the remaining interviews reveal only minor fluctuations. Divorced midlife women show a high and steady proportion participating in the work force both before and after marriage ends.

Although it might seem likely that much of the increased involvement before divorce was among women who had previously separated, this is not the case. Comparisons of only the women moving directly to divorce showed them having the same pattern of increasing activity over the years before their marriages ended. They had virtually identical rates of participation in Time0 (the final interview before their divorces took place). These results support the argument that midlife women, anticipating the breakup of their marriages, turn to the labor force in preparation (Peterson, 1989). Of course, we cannot prove that was the primary factor in decisions to move into employment. Recall that the divorced also have higher levels of education and slightly more positive attitudes toward work, both of which predispose them toward employment. Without other evidence it is equally plausible to argue that the higher employment within this group contributed to the dissolution of their marriages. For the divorced, then, termination of their marriages is associated with a jump in what is a high and increasing level of labor force involvement. The stability that follows this increase may reflect the upper limit for this group, because more than four of five divorced women were then employed.

Fourth, our attention turns to the separated. Because the sample size attenuates rather quickly, only three postseparation measurements could reasonably be included. During marriage the separated women had the highest participation rates, with two thirds of their ranks already employed or seeking work at Time0. There is no short-term change in labor force participation during the first postseparation evaluation. It appears, however, that there is some decline in participation in the second and third post-separation interviews. Again this group showed only limited differences by race in any interview, with black women slightly more likely than their white separated counterparts to be employed.

Given the very dynamic nature of this sample, however, it is important to establish whether postmarital changes are real or result from selectivity and shifting composition. As with income and poverty in Chapter 4, comparisons for more restricted samples (those in each marital group participating from Time0 through Time5), are used here to evaluate the impact of such composition change. For widows, limiting the sample to continuous participants does not alter the results shown in Figure 5.1. There is a larger immediate increase in labor force participation (21%) in the more restricted sample of divorced women, and this is linked to a lower initial participation level (62%). For both of these groups the essential postmarital results are unchanged. The pattern for the separated is highly dynamic. The decline in labor force involvement seen in Figure 5.1 is even stronger among continuous participants who separated. From these comparisons one can conclude that the changes for the divorced and the widowed do not derive primarily from composition changes as the group progresses through time, but such changes may mute a declining rate of labor force activity among the separated.

In contrast with findings for income, there appears to be no unified pattern of change in labor force behavior for widowed, separated, and divorced women. Widows react much like the married women in their gradual increase in employment. Separated women seem to have no systematic pattern of change associated with the suspension of their marriages. The divorced, however, react closer to expectations by adding to their already high numbers in the labor force. This process, however, starts well in advance of divorce and accelerates to an 80%-plus ceiling in this group after marital dissolution. Either there is something unique about divorce as a transition or the traits of women who undergo divorce predispose them to greater labor force participation (and thus greater responsiveness in this area) when their marriages end.

Individuals' Movement Into and Out of the Labor Force

Aggregate rates of labor force participation show what is happening to the groups, but may mask important changes at the individual level. For example, although the proportions working remain fairly constant, there may be substantial movement of individuals into and out of the labor force. This section examines whether it is the same individuals who provide a "core" of workers over time. At issue is the degree of mobility into and out of the labor force over time and across marital categories.

Table 5.1 outlines movement into and out of the labor force by marital category. Among the married respondents there is consistent movement into and out of the labor force, mostly in the 6%-8% range, as the panel progresses. The small excess of entries over departures accounts for the growth in the overall percentage working shown across interviews. Although the aggregate statistics on labor force participation among the married group changed relatively slowly, many more individuals than might appear were moving into or out of the world of work. Only about one third (34.3%) of the married women were not in the labor force at least once during a 9- or 10-year period (from Time0 to Time5). Obviously, these married women enter or depart the labor force in response to a variety of needs and conditions other than changes in marital status.

For the widowed, divorced, and separated the mobility in both directions is somewhat larger, especially around the time of their marital transitions. Among the widowed the pattern of labor force mobility clearly shifts over

Table 5.1 Mobility Into and Out of the Labor Force for Four Marital Status Categories

| | *Interview Time Period* | | | | | |
	−1 - 0	*0 - 1*	*1 - 2*	*2 - 3*	*3 - 4*	*4 - 5*
Married						
Remained In	43.2	43.4	44.0	47.6	50.3	51.7
Entered	8.7	7.5	7.5	6.6	6.4	7.2
Left	7.1	7.0	6.8	6.0	6.5	4.8
Widowed						
Remained In	45.8	46.3	50.8	57.4	60.3	53.3
Entered	9.3	9.6	8.6	6.5	5.0	0.0
Left	10.7	10.7	6.1	6.5	7.4	9.3
Divorced						
Remained In	56.0	65.2	75.5	76.5	78.3	71.9
Entered	13.8	16.1	5.2	6.7	3.6	4.7
Left	8.9	4.3	8.4	3.4	6.0	6.3
Separated						
Remained In	55.2	59.6	47.6	49.3	—	—
Entered	11.4	7.1	11.7	6.7	—	—
Left	11.4	6.2	8.7	5.3	—	—

time. In the first two intervals (just before and immediately after the death of a spouse) more women were departing than entering the labor force, but movement in both directions was high. A year or two after widowhood more women entered than left, but both percentages were much lower. And the pattern shifted again about five years after widowhood, with more women departing than entering. Clearly the labor force involvement in this group is more dynamic around the time of widowhood than comparable change among the married.

The divorced demonstrate the expected high labor force entry just before and at the first interview following dissolution of marriage. This is mostly among women who are moving directly from married to divorced status, rather than among midlife women who have previously separated. Many more respondents enter than leave the labor force at these times. Their mobility subsequently slows down and levels off to rates similar to the married. Because the divorced have such a high proportion (between two thirds and three fourths) who remain in the labor force across time, once the initial burst of activity has taken place there are fewer candidates available for entry. Even with this high rate of ongoing involvement, however, departures are still a feature among the divorced.

Finally, the separated show high mobility relative to the labor force both before and after their marriages end. From the second to the first interview prior to separation almost 23% of the separated group either entered or left the labor force. Separated women entering the labor force out-numbered their departing counterparts in all subsequent intervals. In general, the separated show the highest level of ongoing change, even several years after the suspension of their marriages. Overall, there is somewhat higher labor force mobility around the time of marital transitions among women whose marriages ended. There should be no doubt from these results that termination of marriage may promote not only entry into the labor force, but also exits from it. Movement in both directions is clearly evident, albeit to varying degrees in the three groups and at different interview times. Further examination reveals that only 8.3% of divorced respondents had not been in the labor force at least once during the years covered in Table 5.1, although the comparable figures were 20.3% for the widowed and 15.8% for the separated. All of these are lower than the 34.3% of the married women who had no labor force activity. Clearly, more of the women whose marriages ended experienced the labor force just before that transition, afterward, or both.

Hours of Work

Increasing involvement in a job through working more hours is included among palliatives suggested for the social and economic woes facing displaced homemakers. In reality, a woman's ability to change her number of working hours is limited not only by her personal traits (e.g., job skills, child care responsibilities), but also by the opportunities available in the labor market. Workers, including those whose marriages have recently ended, may not have the option of modifying their time commitment to the job. There are actually three possible sources of change. First, women already employed may modify the number of hours they work at their current job or by changing jobs. Second, new or returning workers may select a different pattern of hours of work than those already employed. Third, changing composition, as women drop out of the study or of the marital categories, may shift the distributions of hours worked over time.

Table 5.2 compares typical hours worked for women in the four marital status groups over time, using four categories for hours: minimal part-time (15 or fewer hours), medium part-time (16-24 hours), high part-time (25-34 hours) and full-time (35 hours or more). First, the table shows that in all

Table 5.2 Hours Usually Worked Per Week by Employed Respondents for Four
Marital Status Groups

| | | | *Interview Time Period* | | | | |
	–1	*0*	*1*	*2*	*3*	*4*	*5*
Married (N)	1,012	1,143	1,093	1,007	845	746	591
1-15	9.4%	10.8	9.5	10.9	10.3	9.9	8.8
16-24	11.4%	12.9	11.7	12.1	12.7	13.3	14.7
25-34	13.9%	12.9	11.8	12.8	12.0	13.1	13.2
35+	65.3%	63.3	67.0	64.2	65.1	63.7	63.3
Widowed (N)	138	167	183	152	110	87	55
1-15	7.2%	7.2	9.3	7.9	9.1	8.0	5.5
16-24	10.9%	9.6	8.7	13.2	6.4	9.2	14.5
25-34	10.1%	13.2	11.5	9.9	6.4	4.6	5.5
35+	71.7%	70.1	70.5	69.1	78.2	78.2	74.5
Divorced (N)	151	181	209	167	108	104	73
1-15	4.0%	3.3	3.3	6.0	1.9	2.9	—
16-24	6.6%	6.1	4.3	2.4	3.7	3.8	1.4
25-34	7.3%	7.2	9.1	6.6	9.3	7.7	9.6
35+	82.1%	83.4	83.3	85.0	85.2	85.6	89.0
Separated (N)	141	158	163	72	42	—	—
1-15	7.1%	5.1	4.9	4.2	7.1	—	—
16-24	7.8%	8.9	4.3	11.1	—	—	—
25-34	9.9%	9.5	11.0	5.6	7.1	—	—
35+	75.2%	76.6	79.8	79.2	85.7	—	—

four groups full-time employment predominates, from about two thirds of
workers among the married to 80%-90% among the divorced. There are once
again differences among the four groups that predate termination of marriage.
The divorced not only have the highest proportion of workers among their
number, but also have the highest proportion of all four groups employed on
a full-time basis. The high hour commitment for the divorced group does not
permit much upward adjustment of work time as an adaptation to the end of
marriage.

Among the widowed there is a somewhat lower and fairly consistent
proportion (ranging between 69% and 78%) in full-time employment. The
separated start with about three fourths of their workers in full-time positions,
a percentage that increases to 85.7% in the final interview for this group. No
substantial differences between groups or changes over time appear for the
part-time categories. Noteworthy, however, is the fact that most part-time
workers in all marital categories are working high part-time hours (25-34
hours/week), rather than low or medium levels.

There is relatively little systematic change in the distributions of hours worked over time for any group, or in conjunction with the end of marriage. Widowed, separated, or divorced women do not move in large numbers either to increase or decrease the amount of time they work during the week. With regard to the possibility that new entrants to the pool of workers disguise increases in hours among those already working, additional comparisons showed this not to be the case. Hours reported by individuals show no major changes disguised by the shifting composition of the working population. Most respondents (between 70.5% and 86.5%) remained at precisely the same number of hours in adjacent interviews over the entire study period. Even comparing women prior to the end of their marriages and five years later showed over two thirds of midlife working women reporting *exactly* the same number of hours across all marital groups. New entrants would appear to be sorting themselves into roughly the same distribution relative to hours of work as those already employed, with most choosing full-time work commitments. Thus increasing the number of hours worked is not an avenue of labor force adaptation following the end of marriage for midlife women. Its potential is limited by the already high rates of full-time involvement before marriages end.

SOURCES OF VARIATION
IN LABOR FORCE ACTIVITY

Thus far we have examined the effect of marital transitions on labor force participation and on the hours of work. This section focuses on a variety of traits other than marital status that may shape involvement in the labor force. It may be these traits, more than marital transitions, that influenced the women's decisions regarding labor force activity either before or after marriages ended. First we turn to rates of labor force participation by selected sociodemographic characteristics.

Table 5.3 compares percentages in the labor force as they vary within the pooled sample of women whose marriages ended between 1967 and 1982. The first comparison is the critical one by race. Prior to marital termination, the two racial groups were similar, with slightly more black women in the labor force. As women departed from marriage, however, the major change in labor force participation was increased involvement among white women, and participation among black women actually declines slightly. Given the prevalence of women of color in the separated and widowed groups, it is easy to conclude that at least part of the their higher rates may be a product of race,

Table 5.3 Labor Force Participation Over Time by Selected Traits for Women Whose Marriages Ended

| | Interview Time Period | | | | | |
	0	1	2	3	4	5
Race						
White	61.3	70.1[d]	70.5[d]	72.3[d]	74.7[d]	74.5[d]
Black	66.1	61.4	61.4	63.0	63.2	57.5
Age at Termination						
30-39	65.3	72.1	70.1[d]	73.7[d]	77.4[d]	82.3[d]
49-49	61.7	66.1	69.8	70.1	69.1	63.9
50-59	62.8	63.6	55.3	52.7	47.4	45.5
Education						
<High School	58.0[d]	58.9[d]	57.5[d]	58.3[d]	55.3[d]	51.4[d]
High School						
Graduate	66.7	75.2	74.5	74.9	83.5	80.3
>High School	70.7	74.5	80.8	88.7	87.5	91.7
Number of Children[e]						
None	62.7[d]	68.5	62.3[d]	68.1	68.6	61.1
One or Two	66.2	69.9	77.5	67.5	77.3	67.7
Three or More	55.5	58.8	58.9	51.6	70.6	71.4
Receiving SS Benefit[a]						
Yes	—	56.8	54.5	60.7	—	—
No	—	43.9	66.7	59.3	—	—
Receiving Alimony/Child Support[b]						
Yes	—	81.6	82.2	92.0	—	—
No	—	81.9	83.3	70.4	—	—
Attitudes Toward Work[c]						
Positive	66.4[d]	68.3[d]	67.9[d]	71.5[d]	74.8[d]	73.7
Moderate	59.9	65.8	67.0	66.1	64.0	64.9
Negative	42.1	70.6	64.3	—	—	—

a. Percentages are based on widows with children only. Sample sizes become too small to estimate beyond Time3.

b. Percentages are based on divorced women with children only. Sample sizes become too small to estimate beyond Time3.

c. Scale created based on the three items discussed in Chapter 3. These were measured at three time intervals (1967, 1972, and 1977) and the data represent the woman's views at the closest measurement prior to her marital change. The 15-point scale was trichotomized, and the number of respondents in the lowest category was small, and reduced over time such that no data are presented beyond Time2.

d. Differences between groups at this time were statistically significant at $p < .05$.

e. Number of children is evaluated at each time period here, rather than bring number of children at transition out of marriage.

rather than marital status. The married group, incidentally, also showed an increase in participation among whites and a stable involvement in the labor force by black women.

The age of the woman at the end of marriage also shows some interesting contrasts. In the interviews just before and just after marital transitions the differences in labor force activity by age are small and not statistically significant. Several changes diminish that similarity. The youngest age group increased its labor force involvement in conjunction with departure from marriage and in the five subsequent interviews. The 40-49 age group leveled off in terms of their involvement. In contrast, the oldest group, whose labor force participation was unchanged immediately after marriage ended, subsequently experienced a decline in participation over time, probably with the approach of retirement or onset of health limitations. This may also contribute to the differences between the widowed, who tend to be older, and the divorced, who tend to be younger.

The results in Table 5.3 also show a clear effect of education on the likelihood of employment among formerly married women. The odds of being in the labor force were higher at each interview for women with more education, regardless of marital status group. These statistically significant differences by education are more muted during marriage, but increase after marriages end. Reactions to the labor force are differential, depending on the woman's level of education. Among those with education beyond high school, labor force involvement increased consistently over time, but the increase after marriage was no larger than those at other intervals. Thus a substantial component of the growth in labor force activity was the result of addition of women with more, rather than less, education. Those with the lowest education even demonstrate a small decline in participation over time. Given the low levels of education among separated and widowed women, this education gap also may account for some of the marital status differences.

The number of dependent children in the household at each measurement point is also used to categorize the formerly married women in Table 5.3. It should be pointed out that women may move from one category to another as children grow up and leave home. Given the anticipated importance of children to the labor force decisions of midlife women, it is somewhat surprising that there are not more striking or consistent differences. Among women with larger families (3 or more children) there are lower initial rates of labor force participation in marriage, which persist across most subsequent interviews. In contrast, about two thirds of childless women and those with one or two children are employed prior to the end of their marriages.

Afterward, the rates for these two subgroups fluctuate but show no distinctive pattern. Overall, the differences between childless women and those with large families are neither large nor important. A related facet of having children is the benefits they may engender. The next two sections of Table 5.3 compare work involvement for widows with children by whether or not they are receiving Social Security benefits and divorced mothers by whether or not they are receiving child support or alimony payments. The results for both widowed and divorced mothers show no consistent differences in labor force participation rates based on receipt of income from these sources. Although either might be viewed as discouraging employment, women receiving benefits were as likely or more likely to be in the labor force than their counterparts not receiving such support. Again, the divorced mothers, regardless of whether or not they receive benefits, have higher labor force participation than do widows.

A final factor examined in Table 5.3 is attitude toward working. The measure is a summated scale of three items described in Chapter 3, on whether it was acceptable for a woman to work if she needed the money to make ends meet, if both she and her husband approved, or if her husband disapproved. Here scores are divided into negative, moderate, and positive, roughly trichotomizing the distribution. During the final year of marriage there was a 14% gap in participation levels between those with the most positive and the most negative attitudes, with women who held negative views significantly less likely to be workers. That gap diminished for the two interviews after the end of marriage. Those most positive toward women in the labor force and the moderate group remain largely unchanged in their participation over the short term. The moderate group shows growth in labor force activity at five years (Time3) and beyond. The largest changes in the labor force occur among the formerly married women negatively oriented toward working. That group increased their participation level, contrary to their personal views, after marital termination. They subsequently return to the lowest rate of participation by the interview at Time5. Attitudes, then, make a difference both before and after marriage. Comparison on the attitude scale showed that the divorced were significantly more likely to be in the most positive end of this distribution (48.7% of divorced women compared to 33.4% of widows and 38.3% of the separated), confirming expectations regarding their more positive views toward women's employment.

In summarizing the information on traits and social characteristics, it is plain that not all women have equal prospects of adopting labor force activity either before or in response to changed marital status. Women who are younger when their marriages end, who are white, who have education

Table 5.4 Results of Logistic Regression on Labor Force Participation at Time3

Variables	Logit	(SE)	Predicted Change
(Constant)	−.606	(1.10)	
Social Security Benefit Time1[b]	.256	(.695)	.061[a]
Alimony/Child Support Time1[b]	−.013	(.053)	−.003[a]
Income in Time0[b]	.098	(.076)	.023[a]
Race (1 = Black)	−.090	(.234)	
Number of Children Time3	.019	(.055)	.005[a]
Age at Marital Termination	−.036	(.020)	−.009[a]
Years of Education	.119	(.039)	.028[a]
Attitude to Women's Employment	.055	(.036)	.013[a]
Percent Income Decrease[c]	.000	(.002)	.000[a]
Widowed	.227	(.409)	
Divorced	.490	(.330)	.116[a]
Separated	−.423	(.315)	
Previous Work Experience	.809	(.214)	.191[a]
Likelihood Ratio Test	63/13df		
Mean of Dependent Variable	.616		

a. Coefficient significant at $p < .05$.
b. Coefficient is per $1,000 of income or benefit.
c. Percentage decrease is based on the income in Time1 compared to income in Time0.

beyond high school graduation, and who have positive attitudes toward the labor force appear most likely to enter the labor force following the end of their marriages. This profile more closely resembles the divorcing women than the widowed or separated groups. From the NLS data it is impossible to determine whether less socially advantaged women who desire jobs are unable to locate them and so remove themselves from the labor force by suspending their job hunts. It is clear from other comparisons on this sample, however, that unemployment or having a job but not working in the survey week is more common among black, less educated, and older women after their marriages end. Equally important, however, is the clear finding that these sociodemographic groups start out with varying levels of labor force activity. Although in some instances departing marriage diminishes those differences, for other traits the differences persist or expand in the postmarital period. Thus separation, widowhood, and divorce affect women's labor force decisions in a complex way.

In order to further examine this complexity, a logistic regression analysis was performed, with the dependent variable simply whether or not the formerly married woman was in the labor force at Time3, five years after the end of marriage. A set of contributing factors was used to explain labor force decisions at that time, including sociodemographic traits shown in Table 5.3, and codes for being separated, widowed, or divorced. Logistic regression allows conversion of statistically significant coefficients into predicted change scores, showing the magnitude of the effect on the likelihood of working. Complete results are shown in Table 5.4.

Nine of the 13 variables included in the equation had significant coefficients, with results that correspond to the descriptive findings. The largest predicted change comes from work history among women who have worked a majority of their time in the sample before this date. The second largest predicted change derived from the variable for being divorced, which also increased the likelihood of labor force participation at the five-year point. Neither of the other marital status variables had significant effects. The remainder of the significant variables had smaller effects on the odds of labor force participation, with increasing age at marital termination the only variable diminishing the odds of working. In general the results from this logistic regression reaffirm the descriptive findings. Being divorced does appear to make a difference in labor force participation over and above its association with sociodemographic traits. The differences in the widowed and separated groups appear, however, to be largely the consequences of their different sociodemographic profiles.

EMPLOYMENT PATTERNS
AND ECONOMICS AFTER MARRIAGE

Key to the labor force's effects is the question of whether economic well-being and poverty are modified in conjunction with entry into the labor force or increased involvement. In order to address this issue, it is first critical to identify those women who were new entrants and those who upgraded their labor force involvement in hours, earnings, or both, after their marriages ended.

For our purposes, entrants are defined as those women who had been out of the labor force for the two interviews prior to the end of their marriages and who entered within the five years after widowhood, divorce, or separation. This definition omits women who only temporarily dropped out of work at around the time of marital termination, and restricts the postmarital period to the years when departure from marriage is a more potent factor in labor force decisions. Although these cutoffs are somewhat arbitrary, they capture the bulk of entries into the labor force deemed related to the end of marriage. Upgraders are women already working at the time of their transitions out of marriage. Within five years of the end of their marriages,

Table 5.5 Entrants and Upgraders: Characteristics by Marital Status

| | | Entrants | | | Upgraders | |
	Widowed	Divorced	Separated	Widowed	Divorced	Separated
Total	25	29	14	94	128	99
At Year 1	11	17	8	20	24	30
At Year 2	10	7	4	24	22	15
At Year 3	4	5	2	50	82	54
Race						
White	19	25	6	58	100	57
Black	6	4	8	36	28	42
Education						
< High School	12	9	6	46	46	45
High School Grad.	8	15	7	38	80	43
> High School	5	5	1	10	22	11
Age at Transition						
30-39	3	9	9	14[a]	50	38
40-49	18	19	4	42	67	53
50-59	4	1	1	27	11	8
Number of Children at Termination						
None	2	1	0	12	5	6
1 or 2	6	10	3	24	36	22
3 or more	9	12	10	16	29	31
Missing	8	6	1	—	—	—
Attitudes Toward Work						
Negative	1	1	0	2	3	1
Neutral	9	10	9	45	41	40
Positive	11	18	5	46	84	58

a. Difference within column in the total table significant at $p < .05$.

they increased either their usual hours of work or their real income (corrected for inflation) or both by 25% or more. Income change can be achieved either by increasing hours or changing jobs. Traits of the mutually exclusive groups of entrants and upgraders are profiled in Table 5.5.

First, it is apparent that relatively few ($N = 68$) of the women departing from marriages met the fairly rigorous definition for entrants. The high levels of mobility into and out of the labor force described earlier suggest that although participation increased, it was not entrants who were accomplishing these changes. Instead, mostly women who had worked in the recent past were once again adding their numbers to the ranks of the employed. Over half of the entrants (53%) moved to the labor force by the first interview after divorcing, separating, or being widowed. Essentially, entry into work and exit from marriage occurred simultaneously for these women. Entrants are more often white, in their 40s at termination, and holders of neutral attitudes toward employment—but differences do not achieve significance because of the small numbers. Finally, not all of those who entered the working world remained there. Examination of subsequent behavior shows that nearly one third of those entering in the first or second interview after the end of marriage had dropped out of work by the third postmarital interview. This suggests that for at least some women the labor force was an experiment that failed.

Among the upgraders, overall numbers were higher ($N = 321$). About half increased their incomes without increasing hours, while the remainder increased both. It should be borne in mind that such changes may have been temporary for some and that missing data on hours or wages create the potential for underestimates of the total number of upgraders. The divorced had higher numbers of upgraders, and, in contrast with entrants' timing, the number of individuals upgrading increased over time for all three groups. Perhaps entry into the labor force is an action taken quickly in response to suddenly increased need for income, while the adaptations to upgrade employment take somewhat longer time to accomplish (e.g., seeking new jobs or promotions, gaining added training). Upgraders are most often white, high school graduates, in their 40s, with small families and neutral or positive attitudes toward women working. Among all formerly married women there is a negative association between the number of postmarital interviews when a woman worked and the number of times she was in a poor household ($\chi^2 = 96.1$, $p < .0001$). Working is clearly important to avoid poverty. The critical question for entrants and upgraders is whether their labor force adaptations have any effect on their economic well-being. Comparisons to address the changes in poverty are presented in Table 5.6.

Here all widowed, separated, and divorced women are categorized as entrants, upgraders, or neither, the majority who made no major labor force change during the five years after marriage ended.[5] Results in the first column compare the women's status just prior to labor force entry to their status in the first year after starting work or job-seeking. Because the income effects may be delayed, the remaining columns compare the second and third interviews following labor force entry to the prior interview.

Among entrants, a majority remained above the poverty threshold across interviews, but there was considerable movement both into and out of poverty. In the first two intervals, contrary to expectations, more entrants became poor than escaped poverty. The small numbers among entrants,

Table 5.6 Effects of Entry/Upgrading Labor Force Participation on Poverty: Pooled for Widowed, Separated, and Divorced Women

	Working Year 1		Entry Time Interval [a] Working Year 2		Working Year 3	
Entrants						
Escaped Poverty	22.2%	(2)	—	(0)[b]	16.7	(2)
Became Poor	11.1%	(1)	26.3%	(5)	—	(0)
Remained Poor	33.3%	(3)	26.3%	(5)	25.0%	(3)
Remained Nonpoor	33.3%	(3)	47.4%	(9)	58.3%	(7)
Upgraders						
Escaped Poverty	13.0%	(14)	5.3%	(5)[b]	7.7%	(6)[b]
Became Poor	5.6%	(6)	7.4%	(7)	3.8%	(3)
Remained Poor	4.6%	(5)	6.3%	(6)	7.7%	(6)
Remained Nonpoor	76.9%	(83)	81.1%	(77)	80.8%	(63)
Neither						
Escaped Poverty	11.6%	(19)[b]	12.5%	(17)[b]	8.4%	(9)[b]
Became Poor	11.6%	(19)	8.1%	(11)	11.2%	(12)
Remained Poor	22.0%	(36)	19.1%	(26)	19.6%	(21)
Remained Nonpoor	54.9%	(90)	60.3%	(82)	60.7%	(65)

a. For entrants and upgraders the years represent the first, second, and third measurements after they changed their employment behavior. For the group who did neither, the times represent the first, second, and third measurements after marital transition, thus potentially capturing income improvements from other sources. Both women who were not employed and those who maintained their level of employment were included in the "neither" group. The first column includes only women for whom the prior interview was not performed during marriage.
b. Differences between groups (based on χ^2) are statistically significant at $p < .01$.

however, weaken those comparisons. For women who were already participating in the labor force, and upgraded their involvement, fewer were poor. Over three quarters remained nonpoor from one interview to the next after upgrading their labor force involvement. There was, in addition, movement into and out of poverty across time, showing no distinct pattern. Finally the group of formerly married women who made no change in their labor force involvement (the "neither" group) showed movement into and out of poverty similar in magnitude to that of their peers who had made labor force adjustments. More of them, however, remained poor across interviews. The comparisons in Table 5.6 suggest that entry into the labor force or upgrading hours or salary were not guarantees of escape from poverty, nor against slipping into poverty.

Remaining out of poverty is, however, a limited way to examine economic well-being. So next the income-to-needs ratio, described in Chapter 4, is

Table 5.7 Effects of Entry/Upgrading Labor Force Participation on Economic Well-Being (Mean Income to Needs Ratios)

	Before Working[a]	Time Interval Working Year 1	Working Year 2
Widowed			
Entrants	1.6	1.7[c]	1.7
Upgraders	1.7	1.8	1.8
Neither[b]	1.6	1.6	1.6
Divorced			
Entrants	1.3[c]	1.8[c]	1.6[c]
Upgraders	1.8	1.9	1.9
Neither	1.8	1.8	1.8
Separated			
Entrants	1.5	1.5[c]	1.4
Upgraders	1.7	1.8	1.8
Neither	1.6	1.5	1.6

a. Ommitted from this first comparison are individuals who were also married at the time of the interview prior to entry or upgrading of employment.

b. The figures in this line represent $Time_1 - Time_3$ income-to-needs ratios for all women in the marital category who neither entered nor upgraded their labor force participation, including both working and non-working women. Thus it is a comparison with maximum potential to show change for the group.

c. Differences between groups within the marital category are statistically significant at $p < .001$.

compared in Table 5.7 by marital status for women who were entrants, upgraders, or in the "neither" group.

For an average midlife woman neither entering the labor force nor upgrading her involvement is associated with significantly improved economic well-being after marriage ends. Although some women obviously do better than others, and concomitant changes (e.g., children leaving home) may modify needs, going to work or increasing labor force activity is not responsible for a marked improvement in economic status.

Among the widowed and divorced women both the entrants and the upgraders show only the smallest marginal improvement in their average income-to-needs ratios after modifying their involvement in employment. Their counterparts with unchanged labor force activity experience no improvement in the average for this ratio. In contrast, there is no improvement among separated women who are entrants into the labor force, although upgraders again see slight improvement in income to needs ratios. What is striking about these figures is that, although upgraders in all three groups are doing better than their marital-status peers, increasing their work involvement fails to improve substantially the average income-to-needs ratio. The

Table 5.8 Results of Logistic Regression on Poverty at Time3

Variables	Logit	(SE)	Predicted Change
(Constant)	−.073	(1.93)	
Working in Time3	−1.338	(.303)	−.237[a]
Social Security @ Time3[b]	−.101	(.087)	.018[a]
Alimony/Child Support Time3[b]	.016	(.111)	.003[a]
Race (1 = Black)	.917	(.324)	.162[a]
Number of Children Time3	.216	(.078)	.038[a]
Age at Marital Termination	.0565	(.032)	.010[a]
Years of Education	−.165	(.054)	−.029[a]
Percent Income Decline[c]	−.003	(.004)	−.000[a]
Widowed	−1.273	(1.28)	
Divorced	−1.991	(1.29)	
Separated	−.221	(.499)	
Top Third of Income Time0	−.685	(.413)	−.121[a]
Bottom Third of Income Time0	.616	(.334)	.109[a]
Upgraded Labor Force Involvement	−.806	(.356)	−.143[a]
Entrant to Labor Force	.437	(.410)	.077[a]
Likelihood Ratio Test	135.67/15df		
Mean of Dependent Variable	.229		

a. Predicted change is calculated only for variables with statistically significant coefficients. Scores indicate magnitude of increase or decrease in the likelihood of the event (here, being in poverty) associated with that independent variable.
b. Coefficient and effect are per $1,000 of income.
c. Income decline is based on the final reported income year during marriage.

labor force, in short, is no panacea to economic distress among formerly married women.

A multivariate logistic regression, used to predict poverty in Time3 is the final analysis to examine the relationship between employment and poverty. A total of 15 variables, including work-related traits, sociodemographic characteristics, and dummy variables for each of the three marital status groups, were included. Results are shown in Table 5.8, including the logit coefficients and predicted change scores for those that are statistically significant.

Twelve of the 15 variables had a significant effect on the probability of being poor in the fifth posttransition year. Important for our consideration is the fact that none of the three marital status variables were among them. This clearly suggests that it is traits other than marital status per se that influence the risks of poverty. Nonetheless, being divorced, separated, or widowed can shape some of these other characteristics, thus having a secondary effect on risks of poverty. The two largest predicted change scores come from work-related variables: Women who were employed in that same interview year were substantially less likely to be poor, as were women who had upgraded their labor force activity. Other important variables were race (black women faced higher risks of poverty) and having been in the top one third of incomes prior to marital disruption, which reduced the odds of being poor. Having been at the bottom of the income distribution during marriage increased the odds of postmarital poverty. Ironically, being a new entrant to the labor force was associated with a smaller predicted change, but toward an increase in the risks of poverty. Table 5.8 reinforces the complexity of the work/poverty relationship for formerly married women. Although marital status variables were not significant, receipt of Social Security benefits or alimony/child support did make a small difference.

SUMMARY

Evaluation of labor force changes after departure from marriage by midlife women has revealed only modest results in conjunction with the end of marriage. With a background of growing labor force involvement by women generally, it is only among the divorced, specifically white divorcees, where a notable increase in activity occurs in association with the end of marriage. More divorcing women were employed, more worked full time during marriage, their attitudes toward women working were more positive, and the differences with other groups expanded after dissolution of marriage.

In contrast, separated women's involvement actually decreased, while widowed women showed a pattern of active movement into and out of the world of work. Those changes net only a gradual and short-lived increase in the percentage of widows who work over time. It is also clearly the case that mobility out of the labor force, which has seldom been considered, is a significant factor among midlife women after their marriages end.

Most women who are already working do not increase their hours of employment to enhance their earnings after marriage ends, in part due to high rates of full-time work. Peterson (1989) argues that any modifications in labor force involvement appear gradually, as changes accumulate across time. The bulk of upgraders, who appear in the second and third interviews after marriage, support this contention. In contrast, the majority of women who go to work do so rather soon after becoming widowed, separated, or divorced. It remains possible that a longer time frame might have revealed additional modifications in work involvement. Thus the changes in labor force behavior vary across marital groups, and the type of change is related to the timing.

Ironically, in recent years as employment opportunities for women have grown the potential for adaptation to the end of marriage through the labor force is in one way more limited. Because it is increasingly likely that a woman facing the end of her marriage will already be fully employed (Morgan, 1980), her options for adaptation are lessened. Thus the opportunity to improve the income situation of formerly married women and to replace lost earnings of the husband are foreclosed for women already employed full-time at their highest potential. Instead of using the woman's earnings to replace income lost from the husband, the families increasingly move from two incomes to one, generally the woman's smaller paycheck, when the marriage is ended.

However, a changing labor market for women provides a wider range of opportunities than was available to separated, widowed, or divorced women in prior decades. This suggests greater opportunities for significant earnings and achievement in the world of paid work (Herz, 1988). Growing levels of education and experience should increase the human capital and earnings potential of women, also reducing the sex-based wage gap. These important trends had not yet reached their full force in the age cohorts under examination here. Perhaps they will result in more women upgrading their skills rather than entering (or reentering) the labor force postmaritally. The NLS women exited marriage during a transitional period, between emphases on full-time homemaking and full-time careers. Many divorced, widowed, or separated women fit the profile described by Bergmann (1981) and Weitzman (1985) of wives unprepared for employment and unexpectedly thrust into the world of work out of economic necessity. For those who are not oriented toward employment or prepared by education or experience, the chances for finding well-paying jobs and satisfaction with employment remain limited.

Finally, changing labor force participation did not create major improvements in economic well-being. Starting (or restarting) employment or increasing involvement did not preclude falls into poverty among formerly married women, or significantly enhance income relative to needs. Formerly married women were also apparently escaping poverty in other ways, because movement out of poverty was also common among women who made no change in their labor force status. The formerly married women who were most economically secure were those already working when their marriages ended and who were subsequently able to increase their hours or pay significantly, a finding borne out by the logistic regression analysis.

Many formerly married women were undoubtedly unable to modify their work activities due to lack of skills and experience, absence of available jobs, child-care responsibilities, or a variety of other factors that might impinge on their decisions. This analysis suggests that anyone wishing to ameliorate the poor income positions of women emerging from marriages cannot rely on the labor force as a solution unless and until the conditions that constrain women's employment and wages are substantially improved.

NOTES

1. The threshold amount for the earnings test in Social Security is regularly adjusted to increase with inflation. Thus dollar amounts for earnings were much lower during the study period and varied over time. Changes in the earnings test provision recently put into force change the formula to a reduction of one dollar for every three dollars earned, but only for individuals 65-69 years of age.

2. Time-3 is approximately 5-6 years prior to transition, and Time-1 is 2-3 years prior; Time0 is the final interview during marriage, Time1-5 regular post-marital interviews with Time3 at approximately 5 years and Time5 falling 7-8 years after marital transition.

3. Data from the U.S. Department of Labor (Report 758, 1988) show that unmarried women have higher rates of unemployment included in the labor force figures than do married women. Data on the NLS variable, employment status recode, was so carefully collected and complete that a missing value on it was taken by the staff as an indication of non-response to the total survey in that year. According to the NLS documentation, coding and decision rules for these variables are identical to those used by the U.S. Bureau of the Census for Current Population Reports (Center for Human Resource Research, 1983).

4. Unfortunately, breaking each group down by race provides some very small sample sizes, especially in the earliest and latest data collection points shown in the tables and figures. Testing for statistically significant differences in such small samples does not present much prospect of positive results due to these size limitations.

5. Figures compare status relative to the poverty level in two, consecutive interviews. Each respondent is categorized for each time period. Those who entered or upgraded their status in the first interview after their marriages ended were excluded from the comparison, since this would compare their postmarital status with their status during marriage, and not reflect only the influence of working on poverty status. Numbers are reduced by this strategy and also by missing data on poverty in some years.

6

Remarriage and Economic Change for Midlife Women

Research has long shown that the majority of people whose marriages end in early to middle life remarry, with the odds dependent on gender, age, and the manner in which the prior marriage ended. Men are more likely to remarry than women across the age spectrum, and younger persons are more likely than those who are older. Recent age-specific data show rates of remarriage of 45.2 per 1,000 widows ages 25-44 and 100.3 for divorced women ages 35-39 in 1986 (National Center for Health Statistics, 1989). Thus in midlife, divorcing women are more likely to remarry than are widows, with both groups less likely to remarry as age increases.

People undoubtedly seek to remarry for a variety of reasons, including an interest in the companionship of a partner, social pressures promoting the "paired" nature of social life in our culture, simply falling in love, or to provide a second parent for the optimal rearing of children. Limited discussion has been given, however, to the potential economic pressures toward remarriage, specifically for women.

It remains unknown whether economic motivations (i.e., need for additional income or desire to escape reliance on welfare) are important driving forces motivating remarriage among women. If women experience difficulty in supporting themselves or their offspring once their marriages end, a new husband may be seen as one of the few avenues available to ensure economic security. Over one quarter of female-headed families in one study escaped poverty through remarriage (Bane & Ellwood, 1986). Alternatively, improvements to income or reduced poverty risks may occur coincidentally with remarriages motivated by other needs.

Because remarriage, like employment, is precipitated by a set of factors in the lives of individual women, it becomes difficult without in-depth information (unavailable in the NLS) to tease out the motivations of women for remarrying. What is possible, however, is to evaluate whether there are differential rates of remarriage according to economic well-being. Higher remarriage rates among poorer women would, if found, validate the potential importance of economic pressures in remarriage, while an absence of an association suggests motivations other than economic ones are primary in remarriage decisions.

This chapter again poses a set of questions to be addressed. First, how many of the women whose marriages ended during the study remarry during the remainder of the 15-year time frame? How quickly after other marriages end does remarriage occur? Who are the women who remarry (i.e., their traits and characteristics) compared to those who remain unmarried? Are there important differences between women who remarry quickly and those whose remarriages occur after longer time spans? Of special concern is the question of whether poorer women or those who experienced a more precipitous income decline are more or less likely to remarry.

A secondary focus is on the economic changes following remarriage. What effect does remarriage have on economic well-being? Does income or the rate of poverty change upon remarriage? Do women who remarry "catch up" with where they should be economically had they remained married? Do remarriages last?

PERSPECTIVES ON REMARRIAGE

Not all of the midlife women in the sample who were widowed or divorced during the 15 years under study here were in their first marriages when the study began. A significant minority of them had already ended one marriage and started another by 1967. Those who were in second (or higher order) marriages had experienced the numerous changes faced by the formerly married, and subsequently located new marital partners.[1] These experienced women might respond differently to a subsequent widowhood or divorce during the study period. Although specific differences are hard to predict, one possibility is that these women may seek new partners more quickly or more effectively than their peers who are novices at this task.

Aside from being in second marriages, other social and demographic traits may enhance or diminish the likelihood of remarriage. If it can be assumed that romantic and emotional fates are unrelated to such traits, then discovery of one or more predictors of remarriage suggests that the determinants are other than random, romantic chance. For example, if women with differing levels of education experience different rates of remarriage, it raises suspicions that forces other than emotional and interpersonal dynamics are operating in selecting women into remarriage.

Here the analysis is restricted to only those remarriages that follow divorces or widowhoods documented during a study interview. For each of these women the NLS data provide clear before and after remarriage information. Results of this analysis of remarriage are not, however, generalizable to all women in the formerly married population. By defining a limited age range, the study captures early widowhood, which undoubtedly differs from the experience of the older counterparts, and also misses the most youthful (before age 30) and the less typical late life divorce. The NLS panel permits evaluation of differences between those who remarry and those who do not within this limited time/age frame, however, and comparisons of those who remarry quickly with women who remarry after longer periods outside of marriage.

RATES OF REMARRIAGE
BY MARITAL STATUS TYPE

Great care had to be exercised in delineating the categories for the remarriage analysis, because some respondents (N = 15) who divorced during the study also experienced the death of another spouse.[2] Some were widowed then divorced, although for others the ordering of events was reversed. Throughout this chapter on remarriage the time frame will be shifted from those used before. In analyses of trends over time, Time0 will be the final interview prior to remarriage, with Time1, Time2, and so on reflecting the interview points following movement into the next marriage. Unfortunately, the structure of the NLS data will not allow following the remarried women for more than a few interviews after entering their new marriages. For many "over time" comparisons, the NLS divorced and widowed women who do not remarry will be cast in the role of comparison group and assigned a randomized Time0, Time1, and so on, as was done for the married comparison group in Chapters 4 and 5. Using random dates reduces the effects of any time-dependent changes in the conditions of formerly married women that might bias the comparison with their remarrying peers.

Remarriage Patterns
Among NLS Widows and Divorcees

There were 140 documented remarriages following widowhood or divorce within the 15-year study. These remarriages were not, however, evenly distributed between widowed and divorced women. Out of 349 widowhoods, 14.3% (50) of the women had remarried by 1982. In contrast, twice the percentage among the 315 divorces (90 women, 28.6%) remarried during the time of the panel. For both groups there remained the possibility of additional remarriages occurring beyond the 1982 end date. Because the rate of remarriage decreases with the passage of time and increased age of the women, additional remarriages after 1982 probably happen at a diminishing pace.

The numbers of remarriers are probably influenced by two contrasting methodological forces. First, the incidence of widowhood was somewhat higher than that of divorce toward the end of the panel. Therefore, the widows had fewer "years of opportunity" to remarry than their divorced counterparts by 1982. More than balancing this trend, however, was the higher retention rate among widows. Standardizing for the number of respondent-interviews in widowed or divorced status, divorcing women still have a remarriage rate over twice as high as that found for widows, in concordance with national data on midlife women (see National Center for Health Statistics, 1989). The rates are lower than expected, based on other studies of midlife women (Duncan & Hoffman, 1985b), a difference that may be explained by the "hidden" remarriages taking place between interviews (see Note 2).

Length of Time Between Marriages

The next step is to examine when the remarriages happened in relation to the end of the previous marriage. Earlier research shows that the interval to remarriage for divorced women has been lengthening in recent years (Glick & Lin, 1986), but remains shorter for younger in comparison to older individuals. Those divorced in their 30s take 5.8 years to remarry on average; older individuals take 6.5 years (U.S. Bureau of the Census, 1977). Little is known, however, about the interval to remarriage for midlife women who are widowed.[3] Table 6.1 lists NLS remarriers by the approximate time elapsed between marriages.

Table 6.1 reveals that not only was there a difference in the proportions of divorced and widowed women remarrying, but also in the rapidity with which remarriage occurred. Nearly half of the divorcing women who

Table 6.1 Proportions of Remarriers Reporting Themselves Married by Each Subsequent Survey

		Divorced		Widowed [a]	
Surveys	Years				
1	1-2	42	(46.7%)	17	(34.0%)
2	2-4	25	(27.7%)	13	(26.0%)
3	5	14	(15.6%)	10	(20.0%)
4	6-7	5	(5.6%)	9	(18.0%)
5 or more		4	(4.4%)	1	(2.0%)
Totals		90	(100.0%)	50	(100.0%)

a. Differences between marital status groups statistically significant at $p < .05$.

remarried had done so by the next interview after reporting themselves divorced (1-2 years later), and three quarters had done so within four years of their divorce. Among the widows, fewer (35.3%) remarried immediately (1-2 years). Widows who remarried had nearly 40% of their numbers waiting five or more years before remarriage.[4] Thus midlife widows were less likely than midlife divorcees to remarry at all and, when they did, took more time to enter that subsequent marriage.

Because a variety of characteristics other than how the marriage ended differentiate these women, the next section compares the sociodemographic traits of women who remarried during the study with those who did not. The focus is on whether these characteristics act to shape the odds of remarriage.

SELECTED DEMOGRAPHIC TRAITS OF REMARRIED VERSUS NON-REMARRIED WOMEN

How do women who remarry differ from their counterparts who do not find new spouses during the study? Several demographic and social traits with potential effects on remarriage are compared in Table 6.2. In addition, because there may be systematic differences between women who remarried quickly (after only one interview), the remarriers themselves are subdivided into quick and slower subgroups. Because the NLS over-sampled for black women, the race comparison is one of primary concern.

Table 6.2 presents two clear differences when comparing the remarried to other formerly married women. First, white midlife women are more likely

Table 6.2 Comparison of Traits of Women Who Remarry and Those Who Do Not and Quick Versus Slow Remarriers

| | Total | | | | Remarriers | | |
	Remarried		Non-Remarried		Quick[c]		Slow	
Race								
White	25.5%	(119)	74.5%	(348)[a]	42.9%	(51)	57.1%	(68)
Black	11.5%	(21)	88.5%	(161)	38.1%	(8)	61.9%	(13)
Education								
<High School	18.1%	(52)	81.9%	(236)	40.4%	(21)	59.3%	(31)
High School Grad.	26.2%	(69)	73.8%	(194)	44.9%	(31)	55.1%	(38)
>High School	19.6%	(19)	80.4%	(78)	36.8%	(7)	63.2%	(12)
Age at Termination								
30-39	36.8%	(53)	63.2%	(91)[a]	43.4%	(23)	56.6%	(30)
40-49	19.0%	(69)	81.0%	(295)	36.2%	(25)	63.8%	(44)
50-59	12.8%	(18)	87.2%	(123)	61.1%	(11)	38.9%	(7)
Working Majority of the Time[b]								
Yes	22.5%	(108)	77.5%	(372)	40.7%	(44)	59.3%	(64)
No	18.9%	(32)	81.1%	(137)	46.9%	(15)	53.1%	(17)
Attitude to Work								
Negative	26.5%	(39)	73.5%	(108)	41.0%	(16)	59.0%	(23)
Neutral	20.1%	(46)	79.9%	(183)	47.8%	(22)	52.2%	(24)
Positive	20.7%	(54)	79.3%	(207)	37.0%	(20)	63.0%	(34)
Children at Termination								
None	16.9%	(11)	83.1%	(54)	63.6%	(7)	36.4%	(4)
1-2	21.9%	(35)	78.1%	(125)	42.9%	(15)	57.1%	(20)
3 or more	22.6%	(31)	77.4%	(106)	29.0%	(9)	71.0%	(22)
Beyond First Marriage								
Yes	25.7%	(38)	74.3%	(110)	44.7%	(17)	55.3%	(21)
No	20.4%	(102)	79.6%	(399)	41.2%	(42)	58.8%	(60)

a. Differences between remarried and nonremarried groups are statistically significant at $p < .05$.
b. Each respondent was evaluated in terms of whether she had been in the labor force for a majority of interviews, both during and following marriage.
c. Here "quick" remarriers are those who remarry in the next interval following their divorce or widowhood. They spend, therefore, only one interview as widows or divorcees and typically 2 1/2 years or less.

to remarry than women of color, with over twice the rate of remarriage. Other studies have also shown differences favoring remarriage by white women over black and other race women (Glick & Lin, 1987). Because the divorced category has a higher proportion of white women than the widowed, race may account for some of the gap in remarriage rates between these two groups.

Second, as expected from prior research, younger women are more likely to remarry than are older women, even with a restricted age range in the sample. Those who are younger at the end of their previous marriages (30-39 years old) were nearly twice as likely to remarry as those in the next age category and nearly three times as likely as the oldest group, aged 50-59 at the end of their previous marriage. Comparisons within marital status groups by age show that the age/remarriage relationship holds at a statistically significant level for both widowed and divorced women.

Beyond these two differences, however, none of the other characteristics in Table 6.2 (education, attitude toward work [as a proxy for gender-role attitudes], whether the respondent worked during most of her time in the panel, children at termination, and whether the woman was in her first or a higher order marriage) made a significant difference in the odds of remarriage. It was surprising that these important traits are unrelated to remarriage. Some, like education, have appeared important in other studies (Glick & Lin, 1987), and most create important variation in the conditions of a woman's life after her marriage ends.

The second set of comparisons included in Table 6.2 are those between women who remarried quickly (after only one interview as a widow or divorcee) compared with those who remarried after more time had elapsed. None of the differences between groups achieved statistical significance, and most of the distributions are remarkably similar.[5] The two variables in which some difference was seen were the woman's age at marital termination and children at termination. More quick remarriages appear for women in the oldest age category and for women who are childless. The small numbers upon which the analyses are based, however, suggest that further investigation is warranted before any firm conclusions are drawn.

In every other way the social traits were quite similar for women who remarried quickly compared to those taking more time to enter a subsequent marriage. The next section turns more specifically to the economic characteristics of women who remarry compared to those who do not to detect evidence of financial pressures toward remarriage.

Economic Differences
for Women Who Remarry

As outlined earlier, there may be important differences for those who remarried, based on their economic well-being after marriage ends. Speculations from prior research that poorer women or those who faced a

Table 6.3 Economic Status Comparisons for Remarried Versus Non-Remarried
NLS Women and Quick Versus Slow Remarriers

	Remarried			Remarriers		
	Yes		No		Quick	Slow
Percentage Income Reduction at Termination						
No decline/increase	22.1% (29)		77.9% (102)		44.8% (13)	55.2% (16)
20% or less	14.9% (10)		85.1% (57)		50.0% (5)	50.0% (5)
20%-40%	24.7% (19)		75.3% (58)		36.8% (7)	63.2% (12)
40%-60%	20.0% (18)		80.0% (72)		38.9% (7)	61.1% (11)
More than 60%	24.1% (33)		75.9% (104)		36.4% (12)	63.6% (21)
Poverty Status Just After Marriage						
Poor	21.2% (21)		78.8% (78)		47.6% (10)	52.4% (11)
Marginal	15.4% (23)		84.6% (126)		52.2% (12)	47.8% (11)
Adequate	28.0% (21)		72.0% (54)		42.9% (9)	57.1% (12)
Substantial	23.0% (75)		77.0% (251)		37.3% (28)	62.7% (47)
Woman's Earnings After Prior Marriage Ended[a]						
Under $4,000	20.6% (22)		79.7% (86)		40.9% (9)	59.1% (13)
$4,000-8,000	29.1% (25)		70.9% (61)		44.0% (11)	56.0% (14)
$8,000-12,000	20.9% (24)		79.1% (91)		37.5% (9)	62.5% (15)
More than $12,000	29.7% (43)		70.3% (102)		41.9% (18)	58.1% (25)
Total Income After Prior Marriage Ended						
Under $8,000	22.7% (39)		77.3% (133)		48.7% (19)	51.3% (20)
$8,000-14,000	18.6% (30)		81.4% (131)		33.3% (10)	66.7% (20)
$14,000-20,000	25.0% (26)		75.0% (78)		38.5% (10)	61.5% (16)
Over $20,000	22.0% (35)		78.0% (124)		42.9% (15)	57.1% (20)

a. Percentages are based on $N = 454$ of women working at the first interview after their prior marriages ended.

steeper decline in their standard of living upon the end of marriage are more
likely to remarry (or to remarry more quickly) are examined in Table 6.3.

Table 6.3 draws the same comparisons as the previous table; between
remarried and non-remarried women and between those who remarried
quickly or more slowly. Of central concern is whether the women who were
most objectively disadvantaged (e.g., in terms of poverty) or most relatively
disadvantaged compared to their status in marriage were more likely to
remarry or to do so more quickly.

Turning first to the relative decline in income associated with the end of
marriage, there are no systematic differences in remarriage rates. Among
formerly married women remarriages were neither more nor less likely if
they had experienced a precipitous income decline in conjunction with

widowhood or divorce. For example, 24% of those whose incomes dropped by 60% or more remarried, compared to 22% of those who had no decline or an income increase! Similarly, women who remarried quickly had fared no differently in terms of income decline than those who took longer to enter a subsequent marriage.

Second, income-to-needs ratios immediately after the previous marriage ends show no association with remarriage patterns. Granted, a one-year measurement of income to needs does not provide an adequate overall assessment of economic well-being within households of the formerly married. Nonetheless, quick remarriages leave it as the only time period consistently available for comparison. Table 6.3 also shows that remarriage does not occur more quickly among women who are poor in the first interview after the end of their previous marriage.

Finally, neither the woman's earnings nor the family's total income in the interview following divorce or widowhood are related to remarriage rates. On these other measures as well, the distributions of quick remarriers and of those taking more time are remarkably similar. One difference that did appear (not shown in the table) is that women who remarry quickly were more likely to be poor during the final interview before their previous marriage ended (20% poor vs. 8.6% among slower remarriers). This raises the possibility that earlier experience of poverty, rather than the short-term changes following widowhood or divorce, might account for some of the differences in remarriage speed. Further examination with other samples will be required to determine whether such difference is valid or important.

Overall, those who remarry seem very similar to those who do not on most economic and sociodemographic parameters. There is no evidence from these comparisons that economic pressure forces midlife women to turn to remarriage as a remedy. Although there are variations in remarriage prospects by age and race, the differences are not large. Finally, those who remarry quickly are remarkably similar to those taking longer to enter subsequent marriages.

It is possible that more subtle attitudinal differences may also be in operation in shaping who decides to remarry and who remains outside of marriage. A role may also be played by chance. In addition, this discussion has thus far focused on only half of the equation—the woman. The supply, needs, and characteristics of potential male partners are also important determinants of remarriage. The next section turns to a seldom studied but important topic, the economic changes following remarriage.

Table 6.4 Median Total Family Income Before and After Remarriage for All NLS
Remarriers and Non-Remarriers by Marital Status

	Time0	*Time1*	*Time2*	*Time3*
		Time Interval [b]		
Total				
Remarriers	$17,403[a]	$22,634[a]	$23,644[a]	$23,298[a]
	(90)	(74)	(71)	(62)
Non-Remarriers	$12,009	$13,443	$11,920	$11,982
	(424)	(360)	(293)	(237)
Widowed				
Remarriers	$10,303	$18,848[a]	$15,472	$17,028
	(32)	(29)	(29)	(26)
Non-Remarriers	$10,758	$11,861	$11,829	$11,709
	(236)	(192)	(159)	(126)
Divorced				
Remarriers	$20,892[a]	$22,902[a]	$23,900[a]	$24,171[a]
	(73)	(57)	(55)	(47)
Non-Remarriers	$14,345	$14,525	$12,466	$12,720
	(188)	(168)	(134)	(111)

a. Differences between remarriers and non-remarriers statistically significant at $p <$ .01 at this time
interval.
b. In this and subsequent tables the time frame is relative to the date of remarriage, so that Time0 is the
year before remarriage occurs.

ECONOMIC EFFECTS OF REMARRIAGE

The final task in examining remarriage among NLS women is to
describe any economic consequences for midlife women. To what extent
does remarriage provide relief from poverty or improved economic well-
being for women in the NLS panel? Do the remarried women catch up with
income levels they might have had if their marriages had not ended?

Table 6.4 displays median values for total family income before and after
remarriage. Widowed and divorced women who remarried are again compared with their peers who did not in order to evaluate economic trends. Here
Time0 is the year prior to remarriage, with women who did not remarry
randomly assigned a Time0.

The results shown in Table 6.4 largely conform to expected changes.
Women who remarry demonstrate an average jump in income at remarriage
of $5,000, followed by stable income in the following interviews. Those who

do not remarry have lower initial household income levels, which fluctuate slightly, showing no significant trend over the four-interview span. Because income change upon remarriage may differ for the divorced and widowed groups, they are also examined separately.

These detailed comparisons show that income increase associated with remarriage is much more dramatic for widowed than divorced respondents. Both widows fated to remarry and those who will remain unmarried have comparable median household income amounts in Time0. Average income increased more than $8,500 at the first interview following remarriage for the widows, followed by some downward fluctuation in Time2. Perhaps the poor initial income position of the widows means that remarriage can benefit them more than it can the divorced women.

Although the divorced women who remarry show an increase in median income levels, it is of a much smaller magnitude than that among widows (approximately $2,000) It will be recalled, of course, that divorced women who remarried started out with significantly higher incomes than both other divorcees and widows in Time0. Divorced remarriers evidence only a slight further growth in income in subsequent interviews. Unfortunately, dramatically diminishing numbers over time as women drop out of the study, encounter the 1982 end date, or experience the failure of remarriage, reduce confidence in the figures for Time2 and Time3.

Examination of income changes on the individual level, comparing remarried women's incomes to their own status in Time0, shows considerable variability over time. Among women who remarried, over half of widows (52.6%) and more than a quarter of the divorced (27.9%) experienced increased incomes at their first interview in remarriage. There were substantial numbers of women who experienced income declines as well, in some instances substantial ones. Thus the median figures mask what can be much more dramatic changes in either direction for individual women who remarry in midlife.

Escaping Poverty Through Remarriage

Remarriage has been shown in other studies of women to serve as a means of escaping poverty. We might anticipate, based on improved income levels, that remarriage would also mean an escape from poverty for at least some NLS women, especially widows. Beyond this, however, remarriage may assist some economically marginal households in moving to firmer financial ground. Table 6.5 compares the status of the NLS women's incomes

Table 6.5 Position Relative to the Poverty Level for Remarried and Non-
Remarried NLS Widows and Divorcees

	Time Interval			
	Time0	*Time1*	*Time2*	*Time3*
Total				
Remarriers				
Poor	17.7%[a]	11.5%[a]	15.9%[a]	10.2[a]
Marginal	11.4%	9.9%	9.5%	10.2%
Adequate/Substantial[c]	70.9%	78.7%	74.6%	79.7%
Non-Remarriers				
Poor	28.1%	27.3%	27.6%	28.2%
Marginal	14.2%	14.5%	15.3%	13.9%
Adequate/Substantial	57.6%	58.2%	57.1%	57.9%
Widowed				
Remarriers				
Poor	37.0%	16.0%	34.6%	20.0%
Marginal	18.5%	20.0%	3.8%	12.0%
Adequate/Substantial	44.4%	64.0%	61.5%	68.0%
Non-Remarriers				
Poor	34.4%	33.8%	31.3%	29.2%
Marginal	14.2%	10.8%	14.7%	12.5%
Adequate/Substantial	51.4%	55.4%	54.0%	58.3%
Divorced				
Remarriers				
Poor	12.3%[b]	8.7%[a]	8.3%[b]	6.7%[a]
Marginal	12.3%	8.7%	12.5%	11.1%
Adequate/Substantial	75.4%	82.6%	79.2%	82.2%
Non-Remarriers				
Poor	18.6%	18.6%	22.5%	26.8%
Marginal	14.3%	19.5%	16.2%	15.9%
Adequate/Substantial	67.1%	61.9%	61.3%	57.3%

a. Differences between remarriers and those who did not remarry within the marital category and in the given year are statistically significant at $p < .05$.
b. Differences between remarriers and those who did not remarry within a marital category and in the given year are statistically significant ($p < .10$).
c. Adequate income (1.5 to 3 times poverty level) and substantial income (more than 3 times poverty level) were grouped together here for analysis.

relative to needs both before and after remarriage. Again, those widows and divorcees who did not remarry serve as a comparison group.

Figures for the remarriers show improvements in economic well-being. Poverty declines, and the proportion with an adequate or substantial income increases. The improvement is most dramatic immediately following remarriage, and there is some downturn in Time2. There is only a slight decline, however, in the percentage of remarriers who are *Marginal* across interviews. It may be that some poor women improve their circumstances by moving into the marginal category, while others on the edge of poverty advance at remarriage to the ranks with adequate incomes.

In sharp contrast, economic well-being remained unchanged for those who did not remarry. Over one quarter of those women were poor, and an additional 14%-15% had marginal incomes in each of the interviews.

In the relatively poorer widowed group there is a more dramatic improvement in economic standing immediately after remarriage, with an increase of 20% in the adequate range. Still, about one in five widows remained marginal just after remarriage according to their income reports. The tenuous nature of their financial status is validated by the apparent economic decline in Time2, as some fall back into poverty. Again, among widows who did not remarry economic well-being remained essentially unchanged, with about one in three in poverty and 10%-15% having marginal incomes.

The pattern for the divorced women differs in some important ways. First, they have better income-to-needs ratios before remarriage, with those who would remarry slightly better off. For the divorced women there is only a slight reduction in poverty after remarriage, bounded by the already low levels of poverty among the divorced remarriers (12.3% in Time0). This improvement is followed by further reductions in the percentage poor in subsequent interviews, while the economically stable proportion continues to increase.

Among divorced women who do not remarry, poverty and *Marginal* income are higher and grow slightly over time, while the corresponding figures having *Adequate* or *Substantial* incomes decline from 67% to 57%. A more detailed individual-level analysis of income to needs showed extensive change across time periods. Women were both moving into and out of poverty following remarriage, as well as between other levels, and the dynamism was not limited to women who had remarried. Thus the overall figures hide a relatively substantial rate of bidirectional movement in terms of economic well-being, as the financial tides improve or deteriorate with remarriage and a variety of other life changes.

Comparisons for more limited samples, omitting those who dropped out of the study during this time frame, suggest that these changes are not due to selective attrition. Although the economic well-being of both widowed and divorced women is slightly better in the more limited sample comparisons, both the direction and magnitude of differences between those who remarry and those who do not are largely the same.

Table 6.6 Comparisons of Economic Status of Remarried Women with Projected Values

	Time Interval			
	Time0	*Time1*	*Time2*	*Time3*
Median Total Family Income				
Remarried	$17,403	$22,634	$23,644	$23,298
(*N*)	(90)	(74)	(71)	(62)
Projected Values[a]	$27,048	$28,142	$30,650	$34,342
(*N*)	(120)	(120)	(81)	(42)
Poverty Status				
Remarried				
Poor%	17.7%	11.5%	15.9%	10.2%
Marginal	11.4%	9.9%	9.5%	10.2%
Projected Values[b]				
Poor	12.5%	12.5%	15.0%	19.0%
Marginal	15.2%	15.2%	11.3%	7.1%

a. For remarriers, these figures are based on a base year (Time–1 when available and Time0 for those where it is unavailable) inflated by 3.8% per year between the base year and the point of remarriage. The inflation factor was determined by calculating the average inflation for married women over a five-interview span randomly selected.

b. Because there was essentially no change in the income-to-needs ratio for married women over time, the income-to-needs distribution in the base year (as defined above) served as the projected value. The changes in these projected values are created by shifting composition over time

Catching Up Economically

A final way to evaluate economic change after remarriage is to compare the progress of remarriers with what their statuses might have been had they not been widowed or divorced. Because there were clear pretermination differences in economic status between these women and the continuously married, it is less appropriate to use the latter for comparison. Instead, the prewidowhood or predivorce status of the women who remarried is adjusted, using a growth factor based on the experience of the continuously married, over the appropriate number of years between the prior marriage and remarriage. These figures estimate where these remarriers might have been in terms of economic well-being had they remained in those prior marriages.

Table 6.6 outlines the differences in total family income and income relative to needs for NLS women who remarried, and their projected levels had their former marriages not ended.

The first panel in this table contrasts median family income of remarried women with their projected income amounts. As we have seen before, the average remarried woman does improve her household income upon remarriage, but the change is immediate and only moderate in size. The improvement in median income among remarriers brings them much closer to the levels of projected income from their earlier marriages. The remarried, however, do not catch up. There remains a gap of several thousand dollars in income, even five years after remarriage.

Turning to the poverty rates, differences also remain between the experience of the remarriers and what may have happened had they continued in their prior marriages. In Time0 the soon-to-be remarried experience more poverty than projected, but the gap is relatively small. Combining poor and marginal levels places the remarried very close to their projected values in the same time period. Upon entry into remarriages there is improvement, with a reduction in both poor and marginal income percentages, so that combining these groups gives a figure slightly lower than the projected value. By Time3 the remarried are faring somewhat better than their projected figures in terms of poverty and economic well-being.

Evidence in Table 6.6 leads to the conclusion that although remarriage improves the income of a typical midlife woman and her dependent children, it does not bring the household up to the income projected had her prior marriage remained intact. The conclusion with regard to poverty and marginal income levels is less clear. The remarried do not fare considerably better or worse than their projected values. These comparisons rest, however, on the assumption that the changes in income and poverty of the continuously married women are valid for these women as well, an assumption that is subject to challenge.

The income contrasts, if correct, portend long-term shortfalls of income, especially given the possibility of subsequent marital disruptions. It may be, as some contend (see Fethke, 1989), that disruption of marriage in early to middle life creates a disadvantage from which women are unable to recover, even after many years of remarriage.

STABILITY OF REMARRIAGES

There has been considerable research attention given to the stability of remarriages, with Cherlin (1978) referring to them as incomplete institutions. Most studies show rates of marital dissolution to be higher for remarriages than in first marriages (Martin & Bumpass, 1989). Remarriages can, however, be disrupted by more than subsequent divorce. Spouses can also die, as was the case for a few NLS remarried women.

Following the remarriages during the NLS panel over time reveals a fairly high rate of disruption. Of those remarriages established early enough to be followed for at least five years, only three quarters were intact at the end of that time. Of the remaining remarriages, most (12.2%) were terminated by divorce, somewhat fewer (7.8%) couples had separated, and a few (5.5%) women were widowed. Data on additional years in remarriage (available on only a very limited number of women) suggest that disruptions continue to reduce the ranks of remarrieds over time.

Remarriage, then, serves as no guarantee of stability in economic or social dimensions of the women's lives. Women whose lives might be disrupted following one marital termination might experience similar consequences again if their new marriages also end. Unfortunately, the number of cases in which remarriages end within the time frame of the study are too small to allow any effective characterization of the aftermath of this event. There is no reason, however, to suspect that the consequences of ending a remarriage would be dramatically different from those already reported here, especially because some of the exits from marriage studied were from second or later marriages. Any benefits associated with remarriage, then, were once again removed for one out of four women within five years after instituting a new marital relationship.

SUMMARY

The remarriages documented during the 15 years under study reveal some important trends. First, widowed and divorced women are not equally likely to remarry, even if the age difference between the groups is taken into account. National statistics show marked differences in the probability of remarriage for widowed and divorced women in midlife, so the result is not surprising. Although younger women from both groups are more likely to remarry than their older counterparts, there appear to be factors other than simply age accounting for the widow/divorcee difference. White women also are more likely to remarry than black women. Given the higher percentage of black women among the widowed, this may be part of their lower odds of remarriage. Divorced women also are more likely to remarry quickly, with a typical widow taking somewhat longer to enter a subsequent marriage.

Surprisingly, however, the other factors that were expected to differentiate between women who remarried and those who did not were unimportant.

Because only age and race make differences in remarriage in this sample, it seems plausible that remaining unexplained differences between the widowed and divorced must reside in unmeasured factors, including attitudinal differences. Further research should explore these issues in greater detail, because the NLS study did not include questions directed toward examining those issues.

In terms of economic status, remarriers were not worse off on a range of economic indicators than their peers who remained unmarried. Neither a sharp decline in income nor a less favorable income-to-needs ratio after the prior marriage ended translated into greater odds of remarriage. There is no evidence, therefore, that remarriage is undertaken to relieve economic pressures among formerly married women. This result contradicts findings of other studies (Glick & Lin, 1987) that suggest poorer women remarry, and do so more quickly than their more affluent and educated peers.

For both widowed and divorced women, remarriage improved their economic well-being. The gains clearly were more striking for the widows, who started out with lower average incomes and higher rates of poverty after their husbands died. Once the initial improvements appeared at remarriage, however, income stabilized and poverty rates show no further improvement.

Comparing the remarriers to projections of how they might have fared if they had continued in their prior marriages revealed that although remarriage brought improvements, the remarriers never caught up in income. Given marital homogamy, it is probable that they again select partners with less income and education. Although an evaluation of asset change was deemed impossible given the small numbers of remarriers and the intermittent measurement of assets, it is likely that remarriers would also lag behind projections for asset accumulation.

Although remarriage clearly presents improved economic well-being for most women and their dependent children, the financial disruption associated with widowhood or divorce may leave a mark on economic standing that is never totally erased. Returning to the central question regarding the economic protection of marriage, there are clear implications from these results. First, the typical midlife woman reentering marriage does immediately improve her income status. Presence of the husband's earnings moves some women out of the ranks of the poor. There is no evidence, however, to suggest that women who are poorer are entering remarriages in larger numbers simply as a means of escaping poverty. Perhaps the poorest women have fewer opportunities to meet men who are likely partners for remarriage. These poorer women are more often not employed or working in traditionally female jobs.

It is ironic that the more well-to-do women, especially among the divorced, have somewhat higher odds of remarriage, because they "need" the income from remarriage less than their poorer counterparts. Finally, data on stability of remarriages argues that it is not a permanent solution to economic distress for a substantial minority of women who unfortunately saw their remarriages end before 1982.

NOTES

1. A small number of these women might be characterized as "marital movers," who have very active patterns of mobility from one marriage to another. Only a few individuals of this type could increase the rates of all types of marital transitions substantially, including remarriage, through their behaviors.

2. There is an interesting sidelight to examining remarriages, because some of them occurred "invisibly." Invisibility here refers to the fact that respondents were divorced or widowed after one interview and subsequently remarried prior to the next. Such occurrences are not unexpected when interviews are sometimes two years apart.

Examining marital history questions from the 1977 and 1982 surveys, however, it was possible to uncover a number of individuals ($N = 80$) who had experienced apparent transitions out of marriage (details unknown) and back into a subsequent marriage between surveys. We cannot confidently describe the situations of the women with "invisible transitions" or speculate about how the initially studied marriage ended. Only those respondents for whom the NLS provides documented information during their nonmarried period are analyzed. Remarriages in the data analyses underestimate the total number of remarriages that occur.

3. Specific dates of remarriages are only available for respondents who participated in the 1977 or 1982 surveys. Because many women had dropped out before these surveys, the reports of the women as to when they were next married during a survey year are used to approximate the time span to remarriage.

4. The widowed women, whose numbers slightly exceed those of divorced women (349 vs. 315) during the panel, were somewhat more likely to remain as participants in the sample. This means that the research had a greater chance to encounter remarriages in the widowed group, even if the odds of remarriage had been even. To put this in more concrete terms, 90 of the widowed NLS women remained in the study for six or more interviews following the death of their husbands, whereas only 61 of the divorced women fell into this category. Thus the difference in elapsed time since widowhood may be an artifact of the difference in participation more than of differential behavior by the type of marital transition the women experienced.

5. The relatively small number of remarrying NLS women preclude statistically significant differences in all but the most distinctive comparisons. Similarity of distributions on these variables is more informative than an absence of significant relationships

7

Outcomes for Women Leaving Marriage: Implications for Individuals and Social Policy

THE ECONOMIC AFTERMATH FROM DEPARTING MARRIAGE

What central conclusions can be drawn from the preceding analyses of the experience of the National Longitudinal Surveys' midlife women? First, the changes following widowhood, separation, or divorce largely support the conclusion that marriage provides significant economic protection to most women in the contemporary United States. Women from the NLS sample, leaving marriage by whatever means, experienced both significant declines in income and increased rates of poverty. Further, once the income declines occurred, the average woman made little significant recovery of income over time (barring remarriage). As Martha Ozawa recently wrote, "When women share their husbands' economic well-being by living with them, their economic standing is secure. But when their marital status changes, women's economic standing deteriorates overnight" (1989, p. 194).

Recoveries brought about by fiscal reorganization of the household, job-seeking, or enhanced careers are not characteristic of most formerly married women, although they do occur for some. These results confirm other studies showing dramatic lifestyle changes, driven by income limitations, occurring in the households of formerly married midlife women

(Arendell, 1986; Beller & Graham, 1985; Corcoran et al., 1984; Duncan & Hoffman, 1985a; Hoffman & Duncan, 1988; Weitzman, 1985).

Second, women who were most at risk economically during their marriages (i.e., women of all races with little education or work experience, with large families or young children) faced higher rates of poverty after widowhood, divorce, or separation. Those most likely to become poor are women with the smallest income or asset cushion during marriage. Because marital homogamy is still an important factor in mate selection, not only are these economically marginal wives less able to earn enough to support themselves, but their equally marginal husbands may be incapable of making up the shortfall. These husbands are less likely to fully pay awarded levels of spousal or child support. Poorer men who die or simply separate from their wives also necessarily leave behind fewer resources for the ongoing support of their wives and any dependent children. Disruption of marriage in many of these marginal households portends severe income crises. Sometimes reliance on AFDC or similar supports may seem more attractive than the slim wages available to the woman, who must also pay a premium for child-care services.

Middle-class women typically fare better in objective terms. They are less likely to become poor or rely on income from welfare sources, except temporarily. Many of these women, however, experience dramatic downturns in their financial well-being. They are, in Arendell's term, "de-classed," losing the amenities and advantages of their former middle-class status (1986). Ironically, in this analysis the women who experienced the most dramatic declines were those who had the highest levels of income in marriage. These women moved from positions of income security to living much more modest and marginal lives. Although most were not thrown into poverty, there was doubtless a significant impact on their lifestyles and future plans for themselves and their children.

Third, it is crucial not to overlook the diversity of experiences among women whose marriages end. Within the NLS sample there are households where the earnings of the wife are sufficient to maintain her after marriage and others that have been totally dependent on income generated by their husbands. Although the overall income trend was negative, some of the women, including many of the poorest, actually saw improvement in their economic standing once their marriages ended. Still others experienced intermittent bouts of poverty and firmer financial footing over time. This diversity is not surprising, given the numerous factors that impinge on the incomes of these households both during and after marriage. Predictions about the average woman in no way reflect the "best" or the "worst" cases appearing in this study.

Fourth, an entire range of characteristics describing the women's backgrounds shape the conditions they face and the options available to them when they exit marriage. It is not simply leaving marriage that determines their fates, nor the manner in which marriage ends. Instead, it is the woman's history and her earlier choices and opportunities regarding education, family, and career that may either enhance or constrict her risks and options once she is separated, widowed, or divorced. Even prior to the end of marriage, women who would face marital disruption are different in significant ways from their counterparts who would remain married. They are more likely to be black, to have lower income, to be less educated (except for the divorced), and to be employed as they approach the end of their marriages. Therefore, the economic fortunes of these midlife women after leaving marriage are a composite of their initial characteristics, the selective processes that concentrate women with certain traits in the formerly married category, and loss of the economic protection of marriage. Cross-sectional comparisons tend to merge these effects in comparisons with the married. The more dynamic comparisons of longitudinal analyses show the changes in conjunction with termination of marriage to be important but clearly not responsible for all of the differences between married and formerly married women.

Analysis of remarriage patterns, however, does not validate the second aspect of the economic protection of marriage argument; that women are pushed back into marriage by economic need. The characteristics of remarriers show no emphasis toward poorer women remarrying or doing so more quickly. Specifically, there is no evidence that remarriage is sought by a higher proportion of women whose incomes dropped the most precipitously or by those who suffered the highest levels of poverty. Among the widowed those remarrying were economically and socially comparable to widows remaining outside marriage. For the divorced, in contrast, the women who remarried were somewhat better-off than other divorcees. It has been argued that an adequate income serves as an enabling factor, permitting women to select divorce during an unhappy marriage and to remain independent following dissolution without financial distress. Yet these findings also suggest that there is a somewhat greater chance for women who are self-sufficient with regard to income to move into remarriage. Perhaps their independence makes them more attractive as partners, or these higher earning women may have more exposure in work and leisure environments to available men. What remains unresolved, however, is whether poorer women are more active in seeking partners or more interested in remarriage because they perceive it as an avenue of escape from financial difficulties. They may at the same time be more interested, but no more successful, than their wealthier counterparts in their searches for new partners. Some other research has suggested that this is the case and that women who focus on remarriage as a means of escaping economic problems also have poorer psychological adaptation to the formerly married status (Ambert, 1983; Spanier & Thompson, 1984). A further test of this proposition, with a larger sample and attitudinal measures, could clarify these relationships.

The protection afforded by marriage is also clearly evident from data presented on continuously married NLS women. These women are consistently among the "best off"—highest average income, lowest rates of poverty, and greatest accumulation of assets over time. Undoubtedly some couples in this category suffer problems, such as bouts of unemployment, health problems, and so on. Nonetheless, the overall condition of this group in the aggregate is much better than that in any of the maritally disrupted groups. Causation is not entirely clear, however. The same factors that promote stability in marital relationships may also encourage stability of employment and financial behavior. The low rates of poverty that are a consistent feature for this group suggest that long-married couples may simply gain advantage through the stability of their personal and employment lifestyles.

Widowed, Divorced, and Separated: Some Contrasts

The results outlined here suggest some important parallels as well as significant contrasts in the conditions experienced by women as they are divorced, separated, or widowed. First, it should be clear that the three groups start out with different profiles. The divorced approach the end of marriage as the most socially and financially advantaged, being more educated, employed, white, and from higher earning households. In contrast, both the separated and the widowed have more women of color and lower levels of completed education. Widows, as expected, are slightly older and less likely to have a young child (or any child) reliant upon them for support. Given differences in attitudes toward women working, the divorced women also appear to be somewhat less traditional in their views regarding women's roles than are widows. All of these differences in characteristics set the stage for variation in the consequences that women experience upon the end of marriage.

Although the divorced start out from the best position, termination of marriage dissolves their financial advantage. The divorced lose the most, proportionally, of all three groups in terms of income. Although all categories of women leaving marriage show notable declines in income upon the ending of marriage, for the average divorced woman it is the most precipitous. The declines experienced by widows and separated women are lower, but still substantial. The result are income levels for the three groups that are much more similar after marriage ends than they had been during the final interview during marriage. The ending of marriage, then, serves as a leveler on the incomes of widowed, divorced, and separated women. The results reported here also suggest important reasons for dealing with the separated and the divorced as distinct groups. Although many separated women do move on to divorce, treatments that suggest both transitions are equivalent (Duncan & Hoffman, 1985b; Peterson, 1989) overlook the prospect of remaining in separated "limbo" for relatively long periods of time. This long-term separation was more common during the years under study here, prior to the widespread introduction of less costly "no fault" divorce (Weitzman, 1985).

Characteristics of the NLS long-separated women closely parallel those described by Cherlin (1981)—women who cannot afford to get divorced. They are more likely to be black, minimally educated, with large numbers of children, and to already have been poor in marriage. These background conditions also render them less able to alleviate their poverty through participation in the labor force. Thus it is no surprise that the separated differ from the divorced in their response to the labor force, with fewer separated women entering or adapting their involvement with work after the suspension of their marriages. The traits of the separated group, which are increasingly populated by this long separated contingent with the passage of time, are quite distinct from those of women who move ahead to divorce. The roots of cause and effect are difficult to disentangle here, even with longitudinal data. Whether they are poorer because of being long-separated (i.e., receiving fewer benefits of child support or spousal support), remain separated because they are poor, or both is unclear. A synergistic relationship certainly is possible. In that scenario separation aggravates an already difficult financial situation, making the cost of divorce seem even more out of reach. These notable differences both before and after separation argue for dealing with the separated, especially the long-term separated, as a distinct and especially problematic group.

The dilemma of supporting these disadvantaged separated women makes their ambiguous legal status even more troubling. They may not be fully protected by the domestic relations laws of their state, depending in part on whether their separation is official and legally sanctioned or merely an informal agreement (Beller & Graham, 1985). Thus the capacity of social policy to assist them is limited by the often informal nature of their marital arrangement.

LABOR FORCE: CHANGES AND CONSEQUENCES FOR THE FORMERLY MARRIED

In many ways the consequences of divorce, widowhood, and separation for labor force participation were less dramatic than anticipated. Like a similar study focusing on only divorced women (Duncan & Hoffman; 1985a) there was an increase in labor force participation among white divorcees, but it was not mirrored for black divorcees, the widowed, or the separated. There was certainly movement into the labor force following marital termination among all groups, but the numbers of women involved were not substantially larger than increases among the married. Nor were there dramatic shifts from part-time to full-time employment in conjunction with exits from marriage. During the same time period, the continuously married women were gradually increasing their involvement in paid employment, as their children matured and as attitudes toward married women working became more accepting.

There was considerable movement into and out of the labor force over time in all groups. Some women probably found it difficult to locate and maintain employment from year to year. Low pay and conflicting responsibilities toward offspring are issues well-documented as problematic among single mothers, but even married women entered and left the labor market for a variety of reasons unrelated to marital status change.

The divorced had a growing involvement in the labor force well before their marriages ended. Both their more positive attitudes and higher human capital predict better prospects for locating and maintaining good quality jobs. This already high rate of employment before divorce, however, precluded much in the way of adjustment to that transition through the labor force. Because many are already employed, fewer in this and subsequent cohorts will be able to adapt economically or socially to their changed marital status by entry into the world of work (Morgan, 1981).

The so-called upgraders, who increased their hours of work or their earnings, should be of growing importance. Although many women will be unable to adapt by going to work following the end of their marriages, such upgrading of labor force involvement may be the more common trend in response to separation, widowhood, or divorce.

Earnings from employment made up a significant component of the income to most households of formerly married women. About one third of formerly married women significantly improved their earnings in the 5 years after their marriages ended. Yet such improvements, through changing jobs or increasing hours of work, seldom were responsible for lifting women and their dependent children out of poverty. It is unrealistic for society to assume that these women suddenly will become capable of self-sufficiency through employment without considerable assistance, including job training, child care subsidies, and job placement support.

REMARRIAGE AS AN ALTERNATIVE

Remarriage is obviously a way out of economic difficulties for some women—but it is no panacea. Clearly remarriage is associated with improved incomes for most of the women studied, regardless of whether they had previously been widowed or divorced. Results show improved incomes in absolute terms, but only marginal benefit relative to needs in remarried households. The incomes in these remarried households approach, but do not parallel, those projected had the women remained with the same spouse throughout the study.

The midlife marital termination may have reduced the incomes for both members of the new couple because remarriages typically involve second (or third) marriages for both partners. Thus, a remarried couple, starting their relationship later in life, may have difficulty in attaining the income and standard of living of those whose marital lives are undisrupted. Whether these remarried women, given more time, ever truly catch up remains an open question.

Despite the improved incomes that accompany it, the rate of remarriage is not as high as those reported from national data for women of comparable ages and marital statuses. Some of this gap is removed if we include the hidden transitions that occurred in the time elapsed between interviews. Although widows were less likely to remarry and remarried more slowly than divorced women, it is not simply age that creates differences between widowed and divorced women. The widows, only slightly older than the divorced women when their marriages ended, may be attitudinally less disposed toward remarriage. We cannot rely on Lopata's (1979) argument that caring for an ailing husband through his final illness was the cause of lowered interest in remarriage. Most husbands in the age range for the NLS women die suddenly from heart disease or accidents, not lingering illnesses. Some widows may simply be more traditional in their views about marriage as a bond for life, or consider themselves unlikely to find a partner who compares favorably with the late husband. Alternatively, the divorcing women may have within their ranks a number of women whose marriages ended because of a new partner on the horizon.

Finally, disruption of these remarriages within a fairly short time period was a very real prospect. The economic recovery associated with remarriage often is merely a passing stage. Many women move again through the process of separation, divorce, or widowhood and the accompanying disruption of lifestyle. Given the continuing higher divorce rate among second and subsequent marriages, clearly neither women nor policymakers can rely on remarriage as the answer to the financial distress of formerly married women and their children.

SECONDARY CONSEQUENCES
FROM ECONOMIC CHANGES

Throughout this book the focus of attention has been on the economic consequences experienced by women when their marriages end. Labor force and remarriage changes have been examined both as having direct impact on these outcomes and as potential means by which formerly married women may adapt to their changed status. But the economic aftermath of marital termination may have many more far-reaching effects on the lives of women after departing from marriage. The lifestyle changes imposed by the income declines at separation, widowhood, or divorce may have important secondary consequences in other areas of the woman's life. In other words, this financial dislocation may affect many aspects of their lives beyond simple dollars and cents.

Distress over money matters may negatively influence the individual's capacity to make a successful adjustment, by compounding the stress inherent in the marital transition itself. The NLS data provide no means of evaluating distress caused by such financial pressures, but such stresses may be a potent factor in how quickly and how well women adapt to their status as formerly married. Another clear example is the loss of the family home, a now common outcome of marital disruption (Weitzman, 1985). Loss of this home, or any economically motivated relocation, adds loss of the neighborhood network, familiar surroundings, and school friends to the insult of dramatically reduced income (Arendell, 1986; Weitzman, 1985). Often the new, less expensive housing is also less spacious, permitting less privacy. Thus learning a new neighborhood, attending new schools, living in closer quarters, and meeting new neighbors often accompany the overall disruption brought about by the end of marriage.

Income constraints once marriage ends have implications also for the quality and quantity of social activity available to the formerly married woman. Research by Gerstel (1988) into the social networks of divorced women suggested that those with children and with limited incomes were less able to involve themselves in social activities that provide potential new friends. These women relied more on kin and old friends, rather than having the opportunity to locate new members for their social networks following divorce. Often they could not afford the dues or activity fees involved in organizations or the cost of baby-sitters (Gerstel, 1988). Perhaps the finding that higher income women were more likely to remarry is partially explained by their ability to afford to participate in activities where they might meet potential partners.

Although they have not been the focus here, research suggests that not only are women affected by the end of their marriages, but children are also influenced. One study on divorce, for example (Keith & Finlay, 1988) suggests that offspring of divorced couples have lower educational attainment, marry earlier, and later face somewhat higher risks of divorce themselves. Certainly both socialization and selective processes provide partial explanations for any differences. It is also possible, however, that lower educational attainment and earlier marriage derive in part from financial difficulties found in the households of formerly married mothers. Thus there may be numerous unrecognized consequences for women and their children that develop indirectly as consequences of the income transition for women after widowhood, divorce, or separation.

HISTORIC CHANGE:
VARIATION AMONG COHORTS

Results outlined here must be understood as the experience of a particular cohort of women. These women were moving through their adulthood in a period of extensive change in family life and in the roles of women. There also were important legal changes in the rules regarding income support programs for formerly married women. Without doubt, the outcomes for the NLS cohort between 1967 and 1982 have been shaped by these changes in ways that may be somewhat historically unique. As Weitzman (1985) suggests, the rules of marriage and divorce changed dramatically between the time these cohorts entered marriage and the time they saw those marriages end, so that the old contract for lifetime income support implied at marriage was no longer honored.

The social and economic conditions these midlife women faced when their marriages ended presented particular opportunities and constraints that may remain specific to this cohort. Their experience will necessarily differ from that of women who went before and the cohorts who will follow them into separation, widowhood, and divorce. Cohorts that follow will differ in ways that may moderate the severity of negative consequences reported here. First, more women are working a greater proportion of their adult lives, even while caring for young children (Bianchi & Spain, 1986). Thus fewer, encountering the end of their marriage, will find themselves with the limited experience or job skills that have made employment problematic for some in the NLS cohort. Similarly, increasing levels of education improve the human capital and thus the earnings potential of women who may need to become truly economically independent at some time in their lives.

Second, as awareness grows regarding the risks of divorce and as more young women observe divorce firsthand in their own or a friend's family, women are likely to be better prepared. By not putting all of their eggs in the basket of income dependence on their husbands, fewer may encounter poverty once marriages do end. Although no one plans on or expects to be divorced or widowed, consideration of the need to develop their own human capital (i.e., advanced education and career training) may replace some of the more traditional decisions to forgo school, work, or training in favor of the husband's career.

These younger cohorts, even with better preparation, still will not escape declines in household income at marital termination, as they move from two incomes to one. Further, continuing sex segregation in the labor force and gender-based gaps in wages suggest they will continue in the near future to be supported on less adequate incomes than they would have with a husband in the household. Women's employment and earnings opportunities, although improving, have some distance to go to achieve equity with those available to men. And women continue to experience pressures through their upbringing and early adulthood that prompt them to forgo development of human capital in favor of the interests of the family. By gaining lower levels of education than their husbands or taking time away from work for the necessary job of caring for children, women still imperil their own economic security in subtle but important ways (Arendell, 1986; Bergmann, 1981).

Certainly the forces for change in contemporary American society are moving toward resolution of some of these inequities. Yet many sources of systematic or implicit discrimination continue to thrive. These distinctions, which are a product of years of gender-role expectations, are slow to change. For example, judges deciding divorce settlements are still mostly males of a generation earlier than most couples they see in court. Some may make decisions on somewhat mistaken notions regarding what a midlife woman will be able to earn in the working world after a two-year stint of "reconstructive spousal support."

LIFE CYCLE IMPLICATIONS

In discussing remarriage and its effects we have seen that those who remarry never fully catch up. But what about the capacity to create long-term financial security among women who do not remarry? The income constraints common to formerly married women have implications beyond their immediate effects on lifestyle. They may also mean that the women are unable to save for their own later years. The resources available to those who remain married offer both a better lifestyle during the middle years and better prospects for lifelong economic security. Many women whose marital lives had been characterized by disruption find themselves with only Social Security benefits (their own or those as a former wife) to support them minimally in later life (Iams & Ycas, 1988). Older formerly married women often find that their standard of living in retirement years is determined by the limited earnings of a deceased or former husband in the early years of his life, and that the options available to them to improve income are few.

Separation of assets upon divorce may also result in a reduction of the private assets accumulated toward retirement security. Thus the marital transitions under examination here can have lifelong implications for these women as they age. Even those with more substantial accumulated assets may be forced to liquidate them for expenses of daily living and children's education. At a minimum many are unable to add to their accumulated value after leaving marriage.

POLICY IMPLICATIONS: SUMMARY
AND SUGGESTIONS FOR CHANGE

The experiences of the NLS women as they exited marriages suggest that systems of postmarital income support for women remain inadequate for a substantial minority of the widowed, separated, and divorced. Simple examination of the poverty rates would suggest such a conclusion. Here, however, the income reductions that increase poverty and reduce economic well-being have been more clearly connected in time with the ending of marriage. After their marriages end, women face difficult choices regarding employment and child care within the occupational horizons shaped by sex segregation in employment, and the disadvantages to human capital inherent in their relatively greater involvement in the duties of child-rearing. Society cannot encourage women to focus substantial energy on caring for children during marriage and then expect them suddenly to be fully capable breadwinners in the event of divorce, widowhood, or separation. Yet that appears to be the current situation.

Both social policies and family norms are currently structured to create the greatest income loss among the women who had become accustomed to middle-class living. Middle-class women, especially if they are employed, often are not granted spousal support or anything other than limited child support in divorce, and they will feel little help from Social Security benefits if their own incomes are moderate or high. The men who separate from or divorce their wives, in contrast, continue to see the fruits of their gender advantage and continuity in the labor force in income that no longer must be shared as equally with wives and children. A variety of researchers studying this topic have suggested that something is amiss in a system of property and asset division that permits some men to improve their economic well-being substantially, while their wives and children experience sometimes drastic declines (McLindon, 1987; Weitzman, 1985). The manner in which the policies regarding money and marriage are structured, then, continue to contain significant gender biases in their outcomes if not their intentions. Traditional approaches for dealing with income maintenance may be inadequate to deal with economic insecurity resulting from life cycle events, such as widowhood or divorce (Ozawa, 1989). Simple approaches, such as better collection of awarded child support payments, would assist some women. Further, research on these awards suggests that many fathers could pay much higher dollar amounts than they are currently called upon to provide

(Garfinkel & Oellerich, 1989). Recent innovations in techniques to collect awarded child support payments may improve compliance, but have not yet been widely evaluated. Regular payment of child support will assist many women, but the problem of low support awards remains.

Additional legal protections following divorce, such as automatic inclusion of all couple assets in settlements, such as pensions and health care benefits, or joint investments in careers (e.g., professional degrees or business licenses acquired through joint effort) may go some distance toward resolving settlement imbalances. The issue, however, is much larger than the simple settlement of property at divorce or the high costs of inheritance taxes.

More realistic appraisals must be made of the resources needed to support women and their dependent children once marriages end through widowhood, separation, or divorce. Child support increases over time, pegged to cost of living, are a minimal example of such a more realistic approach (McLindon, 1987). Availability of generous maternity leaves and family leaves for illness could reduce the difficulties women encounter in participating in the labor force, encouraging more to work while raising children. In a similar vein, equal opportunities to achieve in a wide range of career employment would also do more toward "equalizing the risks" for men and women, but this remains an unrealized goal.

But proposals for change often contain a hidden trap. Many policymakers and politicians are pressed to support "family values," typically referring to the mid-twentieth century ideal of the woman caring for her children in the home. In moving to create more equal opportunities for men and women, however, they promote the independence of women, argued by some as increasing the divorce rate. The trick for society is to balance the equity of opportunities for men and women with the important task of providing necessary care to children and dependent adults within the family. To date, there is a lack of political consensus regarding how to provide opportunities for women to select a lifestyle of the more traditional homemaker form without encountering serious economic risks. And politicians seem unwilling to encounter this touchy subject "head on."

A step in the right direction would be to encourage both young men and women equally to develop their human capital. "Having it all" by combining a demanding career and a family is now recognized as an overload by many women, by still requiring women take primary responsibility for the household and children. Providing adequate supports for their employment would reduce this conflict and overload. Ozawa (1989) suggests that, barring such supports, some women may reduce the conflict and their economic risks by simply choosing not to have children, a decision that could have far-reaching negative economic consequences if it becomes popular.

In pressing for labor force equity and involvement of both spouses in operation of the family, we would recognize that it is no longer practical for families to support full-time workers within the household. We would be required to surrender some of our romanticism regarding the few decades in our history when full-time homemaking was the norm.

At the most fundamental level, ensuring that women whose marriages end do not suffer severe financial consequences requires a restructuring of many of our basic assumptions about work, family, and money. Some components of that change are now underway, but will take many years to bear fruit. It is clear, however, that society cannot and should not accept a situation where some women, and their children, are placed at risk of being cast into poverty without warning or recourse if they are unlucky enough to have an unhappy marriage or a husband who dies.

References

Annual statistical supplement. (1986). *Social Security Bulletin*, Publication No. 13-11700.

Albrecht, S. L. (1979). Correlates of marital happiness among the remarried. *Journal of Marriage and the Family, 41* (4), 857-867.

Albrecht, S. L., Bahr, H. M., & Goodman, K. L. (1983). *Divorce and remarriage*. Westport, CT: Greenwood Press.

Amato, P. R., & Partridge, S. (1987). Widows and divorcees with dependent children: Material, personal, family and social well-being. *Family Relations, 36* (3), 316-320.

Ambert, A. M. (1983). Separated women and remarriage behavior: A comparison of financially secure women and financially insecure women. *Journal of Divorce, 6* (3), 43-54.

Andersen, M. L. (1988). *Thinking about women: Sociological perspectives on sex and gender* (2nd ed.). New York: Macmillan.

Arendell, T. (1986). *Mothers and divorce: Legal, economic and social dilemmas*. Berkeley: University of California Press.

Arendell, T. J. (1987). Women and the economics of divorce in the contemporary United States. *Signs, 13* (1), 121-135.

Bahr, S. J. (1979). The effects of welfare on marital stability and remarriage. *Journal of Marriage and the Family, 41* (3), 553-560.

Bahr, S. J. (1983). Marital dissolution laws: Impact of recent changes for women. *Journal of Family Issues, 4* (3), 455-466.

Bane, M. J. & Ellwood, D. T. (1986). Slipping into and out of poverty: The dynamics of spells. *Journal of Human Resources, 21*, 1-23.

Becker, G. S. (1973). A theory of marriage: Part I. *Journal of Political Economy, 81*, 813-846.

Becker, G. S. (1974). A theory of marriage: Part II. *Journal of Political Economy, 82*, s11-s26.

Becker, G. S. (1975). *Human capital*. New York: Columbia University Press.

Becker, G. S., Landes, E., & Michel, R. (1976). An economic analysis of marital instability. *Journal of Political Economy, 85*, 1141-1187.

Beller, A. H., & Graham, J. W. (1985). Variations in the economic well-being of divorced women and their children: The role of child support income. In M. David & T. Smeeding (Eds.), *Horizontal equity, uncertainty, and economic well-being*, pp. 471-506. Chicago: University of Chicago Press.

Berch, B. (1982). *The endless day: The political economy of women and work*. New York: Harcourt Brace Jovanovich.

Bergmann, B. (1981). The economic risks of being a housewife. *American Economic Review, 71* (2), 81-86.

Berk, R. A. (1983). An introduction to sample selection bias in sociological data. *American Sociological Review, 48*, 386-397.

Bianchi, S., & Rytina, N. (1986). The decline in occupational sex segregation during the 1970s: Census and CPS comparisons. *Demography, 23*, 79-86.

Bianchi, S., & Spain, D. (1986). *American women in transition.* New York: Russell Sage.

Bielby, W. T., & Baron, J. N. (1986). Men and women at work: Sex segregation and statistical discrimination. *American Journal of Sociology, 91*, 759-799.

Brewer, R. M. (1988). Black women in poverty: Some comments on female-headed families. *Signs, 13* (2), 331-339.

Burkhauser, R. V., Holden, K. C., & Myers, D. A. (1986). Marital disruption and poverty: The role of survey procedures in artificially creating poverty. *Demography, 23*, 621-631.

Campbell, R. T., & Hudson, C. M. (1984). Synthetic cohorts from panel surveys: An approach to studying rare events. *Research on Aging, 7* (1), 81-93.

Center for Human Resource Research. (1983). *The National Longitudinal Surveys Handbook 1983-1984.* Columbus: Ohio State University, Center for Human Resource Research.

Cherlin, A. J. (1978). Remarriage as an incomplete institution. *American Journal of Sociology, 84*, 634-650.

Cherlin, A. J. (1979). Work life and marital dissolution. In G. Levinger & O. C. Moles (Eds.), *Divorce and Separation.* New York: Basic Books.

Cherlin, A. J. (1981). *Marriage, divorce, remarriage.* Cambridge, MA: Harvard University Press.

Chodorow, N. (1978). *The reproduction of mothering.* Berkeley: University of California Press.

Corcoran, M. (1979). The economic consequences of marital dissolution for women in the middle years. *Sex Roles, 5* (3), 343-353.

Corcoran, M., Duncan, G. J., & Hill, M. S. (1984). The economic fortunes of women and children: Lessons from the panel study of income dynamics. *Signs, 10* (2), 232-248.

Cott, N. (1977). *The bonds of womanhood.* New Haven, CT: Yale University Press.

Crossman, S. M., & Edmonson, J. E. (1985). Personal and family resources supportive of displaced homemakers' financial adjustment. *Family Relations, 34*, 465-474.

Day, R. D., & Bahr, S. J. (1986). Income changes following divorce and remarriage. *Journal of Divorce, 9* (3), 75-88.

Dressel, P. L. (1988). Gender, race and class: Beyond the feminization of poverty in later life. *The Gerontologist, 28* (2), 177-180.

Duncan, G. J., & Hoffman, S. D. (1985a). Economic consequences of marital instability. In M. David & T. Smeeding (Eds.), *Horizontal equity, uncertainty, and economic well-being*, pp. 427-467. Chicago: University of Chicago Press.

Duncan, G. J., & Hoffman, S. D. (1985b). A reconsideration of the economic consequences of marital dissolution. *Demography, 22* (4), 487-495.

Fethke, C. C. (1984). An economic model of asset division in the dissolution of marriage. *American Economic Review, 74*, 265-270.

Fethke, C. C. (1989). Life-cycle models of saving and the effect of the timing of divorce on retirement economic well-being. *Journal of Gerontology, 44* (3), S121-S128.

Freed, D. J., & Walker, T. B. (1988). Family law in the fifty states: An overview. *Family Law Quarterly, 21*, 417-583.

Furstenberg, F. F., Jr., & Spanier, G. B. (1984). The risk of dissolution in remarriage: An examination of Cherlin's hypothesis of incomplete institutionalization. *Family Relations, 33* (3), 433-442.

Garfinkel, I., & Ollerich, D. (1989). Noncustodial fathers' ability to pay child support. *Demography, 26* (2), 219-233.

Gates, M. (1977). Homemakers into widows and divorcees: Can the law provide economic protection? In J. R. Chapman & M. Gates (Eds.), *Women into wives: The legal and economic impact of marriage.* Beverly Hills, CA: Sage.

Gerstel, N. (1988). Divorce, gender, and social integration. *Gender and society, 2* (3), 343-367.

Glenn, N. D., & Supancic, M. (1984). Social and demographic correlates of divorce and separation in the United States: An update and reconsideration. *Journal of Marriage and the Family, 46,* 563-576.

Glick, I. O., Weiss, R. S., & Parkes, M. C. (1974). *The first year of bereavement.* New York: John Wiley.

Glick, P. C., & Lin, S.-L. (1986). Recent changes in divorce and remarriage. *Journal of Marriage and the Family, 48,* 737-748.

Glick, P. C., & Lin, S.-L. (1987). Remarriage after divorce: Recent changes and demographic variations. *Sociological Perspectives, 30* (2), 162-179.

Goode, W. J. (1963). World revolution and family patterns. New York: Free Press.

Guttentag, M., & Secord, P. F. (1983). *Too many women: The sex ratio question.* Beverly Hills, CA: Sage.

Hannan, M., Tuma, N., & Groenveld, L. (1977). Income and marital events: Evidence from income-maintenance experience. *American Journal of Sociology, 82,* 1186-1211.

Hannan, M. T., Tuma, N. B., & Groenveld, L. P. (1978). Income and independence effects on marital dissolution: Results from the Seattle and Denver income-maintenance experiments. *American Journal of Sociology, 84* (3), 611-633.

Herz, D. E. (1988). Employment characteristics of older women, 1987. *Monthly Labor Review, 111,* 3-12.

Hewlett, S. A. (1986). *A lesser life: The myth of women's liberation in America.* New York: Warner Books.

Hoffman, S. (1977). Marital instability and the economic status of women. *Demography, 14* (1), 67-76.

Hoffman, S. D., & Duncan, G. J. (1988). What *are* the economic consequences of divorce? *Demography, 25* (4), 641-645.

Hoffman, S., & Holmes, J. (1976). Husbands, wives, and divorce. In J. N. Morgan & G. J. Duncan (Eds.), *Five thousand American families: Patterns of economic progress: Vol. 4. Family composition change and other analyses of the first seven years of the panel study of income Dynamics.* Ann Arbor: University of Michigan, Institute for Social Research.

Holden, K. C., Burkhauser, R. B., & Myers, D. A. (1986). Income transitions at older stages of life: The dynamics of poverty. *The Gerontologist, 26* (3), 292-297.

Houseknecht, S. K., & Spanier, G. P. (1980). Marital disruption and higher education among women in the United States. *Sociological Quarterly, 21,* 375-389.

Howards, I., Brehm, H. P., & Nagi, S. (1980). *Disability: From social problem to federal program.* New York: Praeger.

Hunt, M. L. (1966). *The world of the formerly married.* New York: McGraw-Hill.

Hyman, H. H. (1983). *Of time and widowhood: Nationwide studies of enduring effects.* Durham, NC: Duke University Press, Duke Press Policy Studies.

Iams, H. M., & Ycas, M. A. (1988). Women, marriage and Social Security benefits. *Social Security Bulletin, 51* (5), 3-9.

Kamerman, S. B., & Kahn, A. J. (1988). *Mothers alone: Strategies for a time of change.* Dover, MA: Auburn House.

Kaplan, M. A. (1985). *The marriage bargain: Women and dowries in European history.* New York: Haworth Press.

Keith, V. M., & Finlay, B. (1988). The impact of parental divorce on children's educational attainment, marital timing and likelihood of divorce. *Journal of Marriage and the Family, 50* (3), 797-809.

Kim, G., Brehm, H., & Lopata, H. Z. (1977). Income as a resource in the lives of widows. In H. Z. Lopata (Ed.), *Support systems involving widows living in a metropolitan area of the United States.* Report to the Social Security Administration, Grant No. 713-411.

Kitigawa, E. M., & Hauser, P. M. (1973). *Differential mortality in the United States.* Cambridge, MA: Harvard University Press.

Kitson, G. C. (1985). Marital discord and marital separation: A county survey. *Journal of Marriage and the Family, 47,* 693-700.

Kitson, G. C., & Langlie, J. K. (1984). Couples who file for divorce but change their minds. *American Journal of Orthopsychiatry, 54,* 469-489.

Kitson, G. C., Babri, K. B., & Roach, M. J. et al. (1985). Who divorces and why: A review. *Journal of Family issues, 6* (3), 255-293.

Kitson, G. C., with Holmes, W. M. (in press). *Portrait of divorce.* New York: Guilford Press.

Kuper, A. (1982) *Wives for cattle: Bridewealth and marriage in Southern Africa.* London: Rutledge & Kegan Paul.

Levinger, G. (1979). A social psychological perspective on marital dissolution. In G. Levinger & O. C. Moles (Eds.), *Divorce and separation: Context, causes and consequences.* New York: Basic Books.

Lindemann, E. (1944). Symptomology and management of acute grief. *American Journal of Psychiatry, 101,* 141-148.

Lopata, H. Z. (1973). *Widowhood in an American city.* Cambridge, MA: Schenkman.

Lopata, H. Z. (1979). *Women as widows: Support systems.* New York: Elsevier.

Lopata, H. Z., & Brehm, H. P. (1986). *Widows and dependent wives: From social problem to federal program.* New York: Praeger.

Lopata, H. Z., & Norr, K. F. (1980). Changing commitments of American women to work and family roles. *Social Security Bulletin, 43,* 3-14.

Mallan, L. (1975). Young widows and their children: A comparative report. *Social Security Bulletin, 38,* 3-21.

Martin, T. C., & Bumpass, L. L. (1989). Recent trends in marital disruption. *Demography, 26* (1), 37-51.

Mauldin, T. A. (1990). Women who remain above the poverty level in divorce: Implications for family policy. *Family Relations, 39* (2), 141-146.

McLindon, J. B. (1987). Separate but unequal: The economic disaster of divorce for women and children. *Family Law Quarterly, 21* (3), 351-409.

Men and women: Changing roles and Social Security. (1979). *Social Security Bulletin, 42* (5), 25-32.

Miller, D. (1985). The Economic Equity Act of 1985. *Washington Social Legislation Bulletin, 29* (16), 61-64.

Morgan, L. A. (1976). A re-examination of widowhood and morale. *Journal of Gerontology, 31,* 687-695.

Morgan, L. A. (1979). *Widowhood and change: A longitudinal analysis of middle-aged women.* Unpublished doctoral dissertation, University of Southern California.

Morgan, L. A. (1980). Work in widowhood: A viable option? *The Gerontologist, 20,* 581-587.

Morgan, L. A. (1981). Economic change at mid-life widowhood: A longitudinal analysis. *Journal of Marriage and the Family, 43*, 899-907.

Morgan, L. A. (1984). Continuity and change in labor force activity among recently widowed women. *The Gerontologist, 24*, 530-535.

Morgan, L. A. (1988). Separation outcomes: A longitudinal test of predictors. *Journal of Marriage and the Family, 50* (2), 493-498.

Morgan, L. A. (1990). Economic well-being following marital termination: A comparison of widowed and divorced women. *Journal of Family Issues, 10* (1), 86-101.

Mott, F. L., & Moore, S. F. (1978). The causes and consequences of marital breakdown. In F. L. Mott (Ed.), *Women, work and the Family*. Lexington, MA: Lexington Books.

Mott, F. L., & Moore, S. F. (1979). The causes of marital disruption among young American women: An interdisciplinary perspective. *Journal of Marriage and the Family, 41*, 355-365.

Mueller, C. W., & Pope, H. (1980). Divorce and female remarriage mobility: Data on marriage matches after divorce for white women. *Social Forces, 58*, 726-738.

Myers, D. A., Burkhauser. R. V., & Holden, K. C. (1987). The transition from wife to widow: The importance of survivor benefits to widows. *Journal of Risk and Insurance, 54*, 752-759.

National Center for Health Statistics. (1989). Advance report of final marriage statistics, 1986. *Monthly Vital Statistics Report, 38* (3), Suppl. 2. Hyattsville, MD: Public Health Service.

Nestel, G., Mercier, J., & Shaw, L. B. (1983). Economic consequences of midlife change in marital status. In L. B. Shaw (Ed.), *Unplanned careers: The working lives of middle-aged women*. Lexington, MA: Lexington Books.

Norton, A. J., & Moorman, J. E. (1987). Current trends in American marriage and divorce. *Journal of Marriage and the Family, 49*, 3-14.

O'Bryant, S. L., & Morgan, L. A. (1989). Financial experience and well-being among mature widowed women. *The Gerontologist, 29* (2), 245-251.

O'Rand, A, M., & Landerman, R. (1984). Women's and men's retirement income status: Early family role effects. *Research on Aging, 6* (1), 25-44.

Orshansky, M. (1968). The shape of poverty in 1966. *Social Security Bulletin, 31*, 3-32.

Ozawa, M. N. (1989). *Women's life cycle and economic insecurity: Problems and proposals*. Westport, CT: Greenwood Press.

Peters, E. (1986). Factors affecting remarriage. In L. B. Shaw (Ed.), *Midlife women at work: A fifteen-year perspective*, pp. 99-114. Lexington, MA: Lexington Books.

Peterson, R. R. (1989). *Women, work and divorce*. Albany, NY: SUNY Press.

Pett, M. A., & Vaughn-Cole, B. (1986). The impact of income issues and social status on post-divorce adjustment of custodial parents. *Family Relations, 35*, 103-111.

Pope, H., & Mueller, C. W. (1979). The intergenerational transmission of marital instability: Comparisons by race and sex. In G. Levinger & O. C. Moles, (Eds.), *Divorce and separation: Context, causes and consequences*. New York: Basic Books.

Prothro, E. T., & Diab, L. N. (1974). *Changing family patterns in the Arab East*. Beirut: American University of Beirut.

Pursell, D. E., & Torrence, W. D. (1980). The older woman and her search for employment. *Aging and Work, 3* (2), 121-128.

Rainwater, L. (1980). Mother's contribution to the family money economy in Europe and the United States. *Journal of Family History, 4*, 198-211.

Roach, M. J., & Kitson, G. C. (1989). The impact of forewarning on adjustment to widowhood and divorce. In D. Lund (Ed.), *Older bereaved spouses*. New York: Hemisphere.

Ross, H. L. & Sawhill, I. V. (1975). *Time of transition*. Washington, DC: The Urban Institute.

Shaw, L. B. (1983). *Unplanned careers: The working lives of middle-aged women.* Lexington, MA: Lexington Books.

Sidel, R. (1986). *Women and children last.* New York: Viking.

Smith, K. R., & Zick, C. D. (1986). The incidence of poverty among the recently widowed: Mediating factors in the life course. *Journal of Marriage and the Family, 48,* 619-630.

Snyder, E., Miller, J. E., Hollenshead, C., & Ketchin, J. (1984). *Old at 40: Women in the workplace.* Ann Arbor: University of Michigan, Institute of Gerontology.

Sokoloff, N. J. (1988). Evaluating gains and losses by black and white women and men in the professions, 1960-1980. *Social Problems, 35* (1), 36-53.

Spanier, G. B., & Furstenberg, F. F. (1982). Remarriage after divorce: A longitudinal analysis of well-being. *Journal of Marriage and the Family, 44,* 709-720.

Spanier, G. B., & Thompson, L. (1984). *Parting: The aftermath of separation and divorce.* Beverly Hills, CA: Sage.

Sproat, K. V., Churchill, H., & Sheets, C. (Eds.). (1985). *The National Longitudinal Surveys of labor market experience: An annotated bibliography.* Lexington, MA: Lexington Books.

Taeuber, C. M., & Valdisera, V. (1986). *Women in the American economy.* Current Population Reports, Series P-23, No. 146. Washington, DC: Government Printing Office.

Treas, J., & Van Hilst, A. (1976). Marriage and remarriage rates among older Americans. *The Gerontologist, 16,* 132-136.

Uhlenberg, P., Cooney, T. & Boyd, R. (1990). Divorce for women after midlife. *Journal of Gerontology: Social Sciences, 45* (1), 53-511.

U. S. Bureau of the Census. (1977). *Marriage, divorce, widowhood and remarriage by family characteristics: June 1975.* Current Population Reports, Series P-20, No. 312. Washington, DC: Government Printing Office.

U. S. Bureau of the Census. (1986a). *Marital status and living arrangements: March 1986.* Current Population Reports, Series P-20, No. 418. Washington DC: Government Printing Office.

U. S. Bureau of the Census. (1986b). *Money income and poverty status of families and persons in the United States: 1985.* Current Population Reports, Series P-60, No. 154. Washington, DC: Government Printing Office.

U. S. Bureau of the Census. (1987a). *Child support and alimony: 1985.* Current Population Reports, Series P-23, No. 152. Washington, DC: Government Printing Office.

U. S. Bureau of the Census. (1987b). *Male-female differences in work experience, occupation, and earnings, 1984.* Current Population Reports, Series P-70, No. 10. Washington, DC: Government Printing Office.

U. S. Bureau of the Census. (1987c). *Poverty in the United States: 1985.* Current Population Reports, Series P-60, No. 158. Washington, DC: Government Printing Office.

U. S. Bureau of the Census. (1987d). *Statistical abstract of the United States 1988.* Washington, DC: Government Printing Office.

U. S. Bureau of the Census. (1989). *Poverty in the United States, 1987.* Current Population Reports, Series P-60, No. 163. Washington, DC: Government Printing Office.

U. S. Department of Health and Human Services. (1980). *Vital statistics of the United States 1976. Vol. 3: Marriage and divorce.* Hyattsville, MD: National Center for Health Statistics.

U. S. Department of Labor. (1988). *Employment in perspective: Women in the labor force.* Report #758, Bureau of Labor Statistics.

Van Velsor, E. & O'Rand, A. M. (1984). Family life cycle, work career patterns, and women's wages at midlife. *Journal of Marriage and the Family, 46* (2), 365-374.

Voydanoff, P. (1987). *Work and family life*. Newbury Park, CA: Sage.

Weiss, R. S. (1984). The impact of marital dissolution on income and consumption in single-parent households. *Journal of Marriage and the Family, 46* (1), 115-127.

Weitzman, L. J. (1983). *The marriage contract*. New York: Free Press.

Weitzman, L. J. (1985). *The divorce revolution*. New York: Free Press.

Welch, C. E., & Price-Bonham, S. (1984). A decade of no-fault divorce revisited: California, Georgia and Washington. *Journal of Marriage and the Family, 46* (1), 115-127.

Zick, C. D., & Smith, K. R. (1986). Immediate and delayed effects of widowhood on poverty: Patterns from the 1970s. *The Gerontologist, 26* (6), 669-675.

Index

About the Author

Leslie A. Morgan, Ph. D., is currently Associate Professor in the Department of Sociology and Anthropology at the University of Maryland Baltimore County. She also serves as Director of Graduate Studies for the Department and is on the faculty of the University of Maryland Graduate School, Baltimore. She received her doctorate in sociology from the University of Southern California, with an emphasis on the sociology of aging. Her research has focused on consequences of widowhood and relationships in later life families, with research interests that bridge gerontology, family studies, and women's studies. She has worked extensively with secondary analysis of large data sets, such as the National Longitudinal Surveys and the Longitudinal Retirement History study. She has published extensively on widowhood and, more recently, divorce and separation. She currently is investigating small, unregulated board and care homes for the elderly and disabled.